The Cover Design

The above configuration represents the placement of meditating triads arranged around what's commonly recognized as the "Star of David." Yet, the star has a deeper meaning rooted in sacred geometry and spiritual alchemy. The upward facing triangle represents Earth, matter, or motherly energy. The downward facing triangle represents the masculine energy of spirit coming down to quicken matter into life. The center of this nexus of the cosmic masculine and feminine is unconditional love and the seat of true, sustainable creation. Participants seated in this arrangement are brought into a collective, coherent heart space of unconditional love where they are led through an intention to manifest global healing through unity consciousness.

Collective Heart Yoga:
The Science and Practice of Manifesting Unity Consciousness

Jude R. Johnson, Ph.D.

Enlightenment Network
Publications

Collective Heart Yoga: The Science and Practice of Manifesting Unity Consciousness - version 1.51

Enlightenment Network Publications
info@enlightenmentnetwork.com

Enlightenment Network Publications is a division of Enlightenment Network, Inc.

Copyright© 2010, Jude Regan Johnson

ALL RIGHTS RESERVED. This book contains material protected under International and Federal Copyright Laws and Treaties. Any unauthorized reprint or use of this material other than educational is prohibited without written permission by the publisher.

Cover design and Book Layout by Andrew Beers
email: andrew@andrewbeers.com

You should consult your doctor before beginning any exercise program, especially if you have any outstanding condition. The instruction and advice presented in this book are in no way a substitute for medical counsel. The author and publisher disclaim any liability or loss in connection with the exercises and advice herein.

Contents

Foreword 11
   How it all began 11
   What is Unity Consciousness? 13
   CHY as open source technology 14
   What's up with the cover? 15
   In closing 15

Acknowledgements 18

Introduction 20
   Yoga and the Collective Heart 20
   The Practice 23
   Open source technology 24
   Format of the book 25

Chapter 1 - Service as the Manifestor's Path ... 29
   How do you know when you are called? 30
   What is service 30
   Isolation = Weakness   Connection = Power 31
   The secret behind "The Secret" 33
   Exercises for Chapter 1 35

Chapter 2 - Accessing the Power of the Heart .. 37
   Science of the heart 38
   Heart facts 39
   Coherence - The healing song of the heart 40
   The importance of gratitude to maintain coherence .. 42
   Mind based logic vs Heart based feeling 44
   Witness consciousness 44
   When many hearts beat as one 46
   Exercises for Chapter 2 48

Chapter 3 - The Mechanics of Intention 56
   Introduction 56

   Nonlocality   58
   Observer always affects the observed   59
   Biophotonic coherence - We are all light   62
   Scientific evidence of healing from a coherent heart   64
   Criteria for Heart-based healing   67
   Last thoughts   68

Chapter 4 - Forgiving Yourself   70
   Inside = Outside   71
   You are your brother   74
   The most important person to forgive is yourself   75
   Summary   76
   Exercises for Chapter 4   79

Chapter 5 - Manifesting in the Eternal Moment   82
   What is Time?   84
   Buddhist perspective of time   84
   Hindu perspective of time   86
   Putting it all together   86
   Summary   87
   Exercises for Chapter 5   89

Chapter 6 - The Power of the Collective   90
   Dr. David Hawkins and the levels of consciousness   92
   Achieving a state of collective coherence   94
   Mantra   95
   Bija mantras   99
   Targeting our collective unconscious   99
   Our changing Planet: Apocalypse or collective opportunity   102
   The Global Coherence Initiative   102
   Edgar Cayce's advice on the solar cycles   105
   Exercises for Chapter 6   106

Chapter 7 - Enlisting Help From Your Personal Connection to The Divine   108
   Identifying your divine emissary   109
   How to nurture the connection with your divine emissary   112

Chapter 8 - What Do We Want? - Unity Consciousness! When Do We Want It? - Now!   116

The Mayan Calendar: A schedule for the evolution of consciousness   117
The Cycles of the Mayan Long Count Calendar   120
Mayan Calendar and the flow of Information   122
Out of time, Out of mind   123
Goodbye causality, Hello co-creation   125
Acoustic Archetypes   126
Sound is vibration. So is the rest of creation.   127
Unity Consciousness as the Christ Consciousness Grid   128
Call to Action   130

Chapter 9 - The Practice   132

Introduction to the practice   132
Step 1 - Introduction, Namaste Circle, and Inner Smile   133
Step 2 - Energizing the body   136
Step 3 - Aligning the meridians   136
    Karana Kriyas   136
    T'ai Chi Ruler   143
Step 4 - Stimulating the anahatta   148
Step 5 - Sounding the chakras   150
Step 6 - Calming the mind   152
Step 7 - Exploring the heart space meditation   153
Step 8 - Awakening awareness of the collective   157
Step 9 - Collective projection of love and intention for Unity Consciousness   158
Ending the Collective Heart Yoga session   164
Group Configurations   167

Appendix

Alternate Group Configurations for Cobra Breathing   173

About the Author   178

Index   182

Foreword

How it all began

    Collective Heart Yoga has a story, a beautiful journey that we have all been on... but it takes someone to put it into writing. Jude has written such a manual for all humanity to approach Unity Consciousness through a practice that is steeped in the heart of the universe... it begins with your heart and expands from there.

    Our spiritual evolution as a couple was an intense investigation into the self... charting of deep and sometime dark places that ultimately awaken you and bring your spirit to full opening. In such a state of *full opening*, we were blessed with awakened Kundalini. A more unified consciousness became something we could access anytime we focused on doing so. But there's a spiritual glass ceiling you hit when you've cycled through the states of moody questioning to moments of intense blissful connection only to cycle around again and again. There comes a time when you realize that to grow further you have to devote yourself to service. In Jude's quest to be of service, Collective Heart Yoga was born. He wanted to create something that wasn't just a rehashing of ancient wisdom from another point of view. There seems to be a bit of ego involved in that and counter productive to the service that is needed in these transcendent times.

It all began when practicing meditation, Jude and his first cobra breath student would sound mantras in-between their breaths. Each one surrendering to that beautiful place of resonance, the effect was beyond powerful. It seemed obvious that if energy could be harnessed with a group of people converging harmonically the resulting energy would be exponential and the outcome would be healing. The powerful technology of yoga has long been used for individual transformation. Collective Heart Yoga was created as a vehicle for manifesting transformation on a collective level.

Jude comes from an academic background and this new train of thought revolving around service and the power of the collective drove him to investigate and research. His right-brain intuitively knew the practice he had in mind would work, but his left-brain needed convincing that there was science behind the idea of collective manifestation. In his research he realized he could write two separate books on the topics but the totality of both hemispheres finally agreed that one thing directly related to the other. The many amazing organizations similarly devoted to the transformative power of the collective drove this point home and are referenced in this book. In his investigation, Jude came to this conclusion.

> *The ultimate goal is more than just feeling the energy, more than just connecting with others, it's manifestation for the purpose of healing, it is about becoming creative, taking our rightful place as creators. And when we come together in heart and intention for the sake of creation... the power of the universe is behind us.*

What is Unity Consciousness?

The most difficult thing for me is to describe Unity Consciousness? This is a term that has been tossed around in circles of people that also have trouble wrapping words around the concept. Jude was telling me about a conference call he was on with the Cosmic Convergence planning group. The discussion became circular always coming back to "What is Unity Consciousness? What does that mean? How do we communicate that to others?" This made me feel better to know others were having the same issue. I understand Unity Consciousness as I have experienced Unity Consciousness... but translating that to others leaves me tongue tied. So this is Jude's take on that.

> *I realized that the idea of Unity Consciousness can't be communicated verbally. Language is just not the mechanism for communicating on that level. With any spiritual journey it is about the experience. A teacher or facilitator can attempt to translate that experience into words but all they are really doing is pointing you in a direction. But the journey in that direction really has to be experienced by the individual - or in this case by the collective - to understand it. The experience is critical for any kind of common understanding of what Unity Consciousness is. Without it we are going to be a bunch of fragmented individual consciousness, trying to agree upon an collective consciousness that most rarely experience. So the only way to get there is to experience it together. CHY's intention for the experience of Unity Consciousness is all encompassing; all other forms of healing are derived from that. It will target exactly what this planet needs.*

CHY as open source technology

Jude has set this practice in motion as an open source technology. He has taken all that he has been taught as well as the new spiritual technologies that have been delivered to him through meditation and put it all out there as open source technology. The only thing he chose to trademark was the actual name, Collective Heart Yoga, to protect the integrity of what he, personally, contributes. So if John in Atlanta, for instance, facilitates a session it may evolve into something deeper and then one of his participants goes home to Oregon and facilitates a session with another flavor. He may have a whole new experience and post it through the Collective Heart Yoga website… this will broadcast the evolution collectively and the transcending motion of unity healing goes out there completely viral! I am sure there will be some eyebrows raised regarding the release of such techniques… opening Pandora's box so to speak. In the guru-to-student dynamic there are financial gains to be had… and, yes, there is validity to not giving a student too much too fast. But the meteoric pace of technology and spiritual awakening makes this no longer a factor, especially to our readers… those who will be magnetized to Collective Heart Yoga. I asked Jude to describe his intention to allow this information to be free flowing.

I have always loved the idea of open source technology; it has evolved because of the democracy of information on the internet. The most robust and creative software and websites such as Linux OS or Wikipedia… are all completely transparent and are completely open to all useful contributions. Nothing is hidden, no more withholding of information for financial gain. The power of the masses can help the practice of Collective Heart Yoga evolve far faster than it could if one individual or small elite group claimed ownership and controlled access to the wisdom and practice. How can you really own or control what you teach to others... anyway? Your cache in the "New Economy" is not what you own but what you offer and the integrity in which you offer it.

What's up with the cover?

The book cover... speaks volumes to what you will find beyond these pages and is a reflection of the actual practice. I received the draft along with many other friends, family members, and colleagues. The response that was most prevalent seemed to be "I love the flower of life" or "Why are the meditators on the star of David?" I knew there was a deeper connection than that... so again I went to the source and asked Jude why the specific arrangement of meditators, what is the symbolism of the star and how does that tie into the practice?

> *The star is a 2 dimensional representation of a 3 dimensional tetrahedron. It may be recognizable as the Star of David, yet symbolizes something much more profound... it is sacred geometry. A triangle is the most stable arrangement of energies. If you have 3 legs coming together like a tripod, for instance, it is the most simple and stable way to hold a camera. When you put two triangles together, one inverted over the other, you have created something with universal value. The triangle pointing downward represents the masculine energy of spirit and the triangle pointing upward represents the feminine, mother energy of Earth. The integration of the inverted triangles in terms of tantra ... is where creation happens. The inside of this nexus is unconditional love. That is why no sustainable creation happens without the unconditional love of a coherent heart... but imagine what you can do with 18 hearts in coherence!*

So, for me I see 6 pods of 3 people sitting back to back on a 6-point star. In the practice all the energy of these 18 individuals is being transmuted up through that nexus in the middle... how powerful is that? Not only are you experiencing your pod of 3 and its nexus, but the collective energies of everyone and the synergy of the nexus in the middle! I asked Jude how he arrived at this arrangement?

Having done a Level 3 Ipsalu Tantra workshop with Bodhi Avanasha, there was a breath that involved two people back to back... Bodhi lead the breath with a caveat to choose your partner wisely as you will have an everlasting connection."

When Jude returned we engaged in the breath back to back in a sweet meadow... it was incredibly powerful and I understood the gravity of the warning she was giving. Investigating further, Jude began to understand why this would happen. There is a synchronization of the nervous system of the participants that could be misinterpreted as romantic love... but an arrangement of three more freely allows the possibility of true alchemy. When performing the cobra breath sitting back to back in triangular seating everyone is synchronizing their nervous system without the idea of romantic attachment.

In closing

It is clear that Jude's motivation to write the book is for the reader to have enough truth resound within them to be compelled to do the practice with others and through that experience... further cement the expression of Unity Consciousness on a deeper, collective level. This practice was created as a basic foundation... as nothing is static, everything is in evolution and we are transcending with every breath... it makes sense that this book is a starting point. As we collec-

The Science and Practice of Manifesting Unity Consciousness

tively evolve so will this practice. It will branch and grow into many forms that will be offered by collectives everywhere. It is to be shared and exchanged... molding our conscious efforts into a broader and expanded dimension. I look forward to sharing a triad with you.

Asheville, NC, U.S.A.					Connie M. Johnson
October 2010

Dedicated to You, The Seeker

Acknowledgments

I am deeply indebted to Connie Johnson, for her support on this project, including editing of this book and advisement on the actual practice. Connie and I both started this journey years ago when we had our first, shared Kundalini awakening. Our journey of spiritual evolution has been greatly accelerated ever since.

Thank you to all the bold pioneers who are studying the connection between consciousness and manifestation including the folks at the Global Coherence Initiative, specifically to Rollin Mcraty, Ph.D. and Annette Deyhle Ph.D. for their ground breaking work to prove that collectively humanity can emotionally access and affect the basic energetic processes of our planet.

A specific thanks to Gregg Braden, Carl Calleman, Lynne McTaggart, Susan Joy Rennison, and David Wilcock, for their profound abilities to translate recent scientific revelations into understandable, relevant, and timely wisdom for the mainstream public. Your writing has been an inspiring model to emulate.

Thank you, Marc Arno, for helping tame my sometime complex verbiage into lucid flowing communication. What a wonderful, enlightened editor you have been.

The Science and Practice of Manifesting Unity Consciousness

Thanks to Andrew Beers, for greatly assisting in laying out this book and designing the cover for publication. He really believed in the project and even though it has never been mentioned between us... I know you gave me one heck of a deal for all the superb, talented work you offered.

Thanks to my biological mother, Maureen Regan, who for the last 18 years has reminded me of my connection to Mother Earth and the rest of humanity.

With a heavy heart, I would like to thank, my biological father, the late, great Tommy Thompson, who passed on to me his love for music and unquenchable thirst for truth.

I would also like to express the deepest gratitude to the spiritual father in my life, Sunyata Saraswati. I have felt nothing but profound love from this man ever since I interviewed him for the Enlightenment Network. Master Sunyata offered the most valuable gift he could give ... the four levels of Cosmic Cobra Breath and the Tantric Cobra Breath. The daily practice of these breaths has given me both the grace and divine inspiration to live as a true expression of love. As a teacher, Sunyata has given unselfishly from his heart for the sake of planetary evolution.

Introduction

Yoga and the Collective Heart

Yoga, in Sanskrit, means to join or to yoke together. As a traditional spiritual practice, yoga defined the joining of the physical body, emotional body, and spiritual body. But this practice has been for the most part a personal practice. What if yoga could be a *direct* mechanism for joining all of us? The changing energies of planetary consciousness are making it possible to embrace a practice for the collective organism called Mankind. The science and practices explored in this book are all about the alignment of the collective body, the collective mind, and the collective spirit all for the sake of projecting the collective, healing intention of Unity Consciousness - that shared awareness that we are all, indeed, one.

There are some purist, however, who believe that yoga was meant as a rigid, unevolving tool for personal evolution. Yet Yoga has evolved in the West whether we intended it to or not. Yoga in the West started with a few beautiful souls in the 60's trying to teach in purity what they learned in the East. Our culture's journey with yoga began by looking at yoga as an esoteric way of developing our precious bodies. We enjoyed how it made us feel but were hesitant to examine yoga's promise of spiritual development. Now, fifty years later, there are countless serious practitioners of the most advanced practices including tantra. And most of our practices are very different from what they look like in the East. There are no sacred cows... even in yoga. The goal of spiritual development is to be completely detached and that ultimately means being detached from the *Practice*.

Many of us have reached the limits of our personal practice. At some point in everyone's evolution the practice becomes trivial next to the call for service. Service is the one plateau in the spiritual landscape that many of us have trouble reaching. It calls for a very intimate surrender of self. The state of universal affairs now dictates that we actively reach out to the very core of the *Other* to realize the *Self*. Collective Heart Yoga is a way to energetically practice that surrender of self in the light of service. It is a way to *feel* at our core the connection that we all share. In this *connection* is the power to change world. It is the Universe's graduation gift for getting beyond the illusion of the individual.

Yet, the very idea of making yoga a truly collective practice has apparently ruffled some feathers in the traditional yogic community. *"These practices are of a personal nature and have been around for thousands of years and they are effective. Who are you to defile what is sacred?"* Yet it has been almost 26 thousand years since humanity has faced anything close to the transformation of consciousness we are currently navigating. A personal practice was perfect for a small, more evolved percentage of humanity. Many powerful tantric practices were kept secret because both the practice and the practitioners were not safe in a world that was hostile to the evolution of consciousness. Yet today, the world is far more populated with souls evolved enough to embrace their energetic bodies. In fact, there are enough experienced personal practitioners to finally embrace a collective practice.

Collective energetic practice is not new. Some of the most ancient cultures like some Native Americans and Africans are very skilled at entraining the group mind of their people toward manifesting common objectives. Activities once thought primal, such as dancing, drumming, and chanting are in reality ingenious ways of tapping and molding the collective conscious of a tribe. You can see vestiges of this in today's kirtans but rarely is the collective manifesting power of kirtans realized by either the practitioners or teachers.

Yoga is actually a technology, meaning it produces reliable results if done with proper precision and intent. This yogic practice specifically uses powerful and safe non-sexual tantric kriya techniques. The techniques are so powerful that, within 3 hours, a trained facilitator with the proper intent can bring a disjointed class into a unified, coherent collective projecting a focused intention for Unity Consciousness straight from the heart.

In our modern world, the current trend of technology is to virtualize as many aspects of our existence as possible. This essentially equates to taking what is naturally analogue, fractal, and holographic and sampling it all into ones and zeros. Yet I believe that, historically, our technologies have been nothing but child toys training us for the ultimate technology... *consciousness*.

In fact, all our technology to date has paralleled what has always been possible on the etheric level. For example, the way we create virtual worlds out of the simple duality of ones and zeros represents the male and female aspects of universal creation. We have always participated in this universal creation, although, for the most part, unconsciously and without awareness. Another example of our current technology paralleling the etheric is the internet, which essentially mirrors the neural, interconnected nature of humanity's own collective consciousness.

To bring the technology point home, our most basic nature as a species can be distilled down to one activity... creation. Our minds have been creating ever since we discovered how to hone tools out of stone and draw figures in caves. Yet, so far, our minds have been limited to what our hands or the machines we make with our hands can create in the physical world. Now, with computers, that act of creation is extended into the virtual world. The science of this book is to affirm the fact that our ability to create extends far beyond what we currently believe is possible. And what is possible within a collective setting can transform this planet.

The Practice

The practice outlined in this book is but one approach to unifying a group for the purpose of projecting a coherent intention for Unity Consciousness. If you had any hopes of using this practice to get *stuff* you should put this book down immediately and look for a practice that stresses more individual manifestation. Manifesting from the heart in a collective setting can only produce one result... *healing of the collective.* In this case the intent is for Unity Consciousness. We will go more in depth about what exactly Unity Consciousness is in Chapter 8.

These strategies are tantric in approach because they powerfully direct kundalini, or your most creative life-force energy, through energetic channels of the body (the chakras) through proven techniques of pranayam (breathing), vibration using sound (mantra), and the visualization of sacred vibration through Yantra, or symbolic imagery of sound.

I deliberately chose to use non-sexual tantric techniques because of the profound emotional issues sexuality raises. In addition, the majority of communities that practice tantra here in the West remain stuck in the first three chakras, repeatedly dealing with personal issues of security, physical gratification, and power. Unfortunately, many never access their heart in any sustainable fashion. It is true that sexual tantra can be a rocket ship to Enlightenment, but only for those who can resist the temptations of the ego that go along with the practice.

These esoteric, non-sexual tantric techniques, in a collective setting, entrain a group toward a coherent, amplified, heart-based vibration with the shared intention for Unity Consciousness. From the curious yoga novice to the advanced tantrika, all will be lifted together to a heart space that most of humanity rarely get to experience.

Open Source Technology

I chose to include the entire practice in the book rather than teaching it to only those who attend the workshops. Most of the techniques are ancient and open to public knowledge. However, some of these techniques - like the Emanating Heart Cobra and the Manifestation Cobra - were given to me in deep meditation. As a consequence, these breaths were divinely inspired and meant to be shared with all of you.

The days of secret wisdom and practices are over. Such wisdom was made secretive because of the institutional persecution of those who understood the power of consciousness. Today there is little chance for persecution, not to mention the world is now making an evolutionary quantum leap and is desperately in need of this wisdom.

Some may argue that such powerful breaths were kept secret because of the harm they could inflict on the practitioner. And let's not forget the harm the practitioner could do to others. I can agree somewhat with such concerns. However, Collective Heart Yoga (CHY) is completely heart-centered, therefore no harm can be done to the practitioner. In fact, the practitioner would be hard-pressed to use it to hurt others. So I present this practice and all the science behind the practice as open source technology for you to tweak or reengineer for the sake of its evolution and dissemination. My one humble request, however, is that you post your tried and tested revisions for everyone else to see and share at www.Collective-HeartYoga.org.

Format of the Book

- Chapter 1 – Examines the spiritual *glass ceiling* that many current practitioners experience within the confines of a personal practice. One reliable path to getting beyond that glass ceiling is through service. The practice of Collective Heart Yoga (CHY) turns the personal practice into a unified practice of service whose intention is to manifest Unity Consciousness.

- Chapter 2 – Explores how the coherent heart can manifest healing on a personal level and how bringing individual coherent hearts together in a collective state can greatly amplify the healing intentions of any group.

- Chapter 3 – Briefly explains the scientific validation behind the healing power of heart-based intention. Don't worry, there is absolutely no math and I have done my best to explain the physics behind intention in the most basic of terms. Yet it is not necessary for a practitioner of CHY to understand the science behind all of this. This chapter is more for those who still need their left brain's scientific nod of approval to believe in their power to manifest global healing and the attainment of Unity Consciousness. Those who feel very rooted in their faith to manifest may feel free to skip both this chapter and chapter 2.

- Chapter 4 – Explains the basic framework of true forgiveness. Psychologically, forgiveness is the conscious practice of internal locus of control, meaning that you are responsible for everything that happens in your life. The practice of forgiveness establishes an empowered mind-set that allows the deliberate projection of intent that changes one's personal reality. Spiritually, it is absolutely necessary to be grounded in the personal empowerment offered by forgiveness before you can come together with others for the sake of creating change on a collective level.

- Chapter 5 – Explores the concept of time in western culture and how such a time-bound perspective limits us to rigid cause and effect explanations of everyday reality. Adapting a more traditional eastern perspective frees us to manifest an equally valid reality without the time-bound construct of one event being necessary to cause another.

- Chapter 6 – Describes how we as individuals are really acting from one single, global, collective unconscious as described by Carl Jung. This collective unconscious is greatly influenced by those of us who are operating on the consciousness level of Love. A critical mass of souls at this level of consciousness can move the entire collective unconscious of mankind toward Unconditional Love, creating a Unity Consciousness rather than our current fragmented consciousness. This chapter briefly describes how the regular practice of CHY focuses and amplifies the intention of the collective through entrainment using rhythm, resonant mantra, and sacred geometry. Finally, scientific evidence from the Global Coherence Initiative is offered to affirm that, collectively, humans can indeed influence the very nature of Earth's environment.

- Chapter 7 – Tackles the very necessary personal connections to the Divine, such as Saints, Avatars, and Angels, and how critical these entities can be in helping us bridge the gap between what we *believe* we are each currently capable of manifesting, and what we *know* the Divine is capable of manifesting. The hierarchy of these entities are, in fact, determined by their level of altruistic service to mankind. This chapter also briefly outlines basic practices that nurture our relationship with these entities and gives clues on how to recognize which entity may be *your* personal connection to the Divine.

- Chapter 8 – Explains the ultimate purpose behind CHY... Unity Consciousness. This consciousness is explained in terms of the Mayan Long Count Calendar and the 9 underworlds of consciousness spanning the approximately 16 billion year conscious evolution of the universe - beginning from the Big Bang and culminating in a rapid ascent toward Unity Consciousness beginning on or near March 2011. This chapter is essentially a very brief distillation of the ground breaking work of Dr. Carl Calleman, and underlines the impending urgency to achieve Unity Consciousness within a limited window of time while the planet herself supports this vibrational level of consciousness.

- Chapter 9 – is the collective practice outlined in a step by step format for any group to follow, adapt, improve and share.

Service as the Manifestor's Path

If you are reading this book, chances are you have been following a spiritual path long enough to catch glimpses of your own power as a creator. This is an inevitable step on a wonderful journey that ultimately propels us into the realm of Angels and fledgling designers of universes.

Yet, built into every personal universe is a fail-safe which informs us that self-awareness alone will not grant us access to our true creative power. We must first become tangibly aware of our connections to each other and to every other living thing. This is God's safeguard to prevent the lazy, the selfish, and the charlatans from ruining creation. Perhaps some must experience great suffering. Fortunate others may simply be touched by grace. For most of us, *service* is the only other proven path to reach that tangible connection to others.

Much of our time as spiritual seekers is invested in improving our selves, conquering our own fears and limitations, and extolling our beliefs, all in the hope we might be rewarded with even a brief glimpse of unity with The Divine.

However, during this time of massive transformation, if we overstay our welcome in this introspective stage of personal improvement we begin to believe that we are growing superior to the others around us who remain relatively unawakened. We become more deeply identified with an ego that has simply exchanged its casual look for more spiritual garments. In other words, we rarely get beyond our selves and the evolution of our consciousness comes to a screeching halt. We repeatedly hit a glass ceiling blocking any further personal growth until we come to embrace service as a new cornerstone of our chosen path.

How do you know when you are called?

You may have recently felt this call to serve because Mother Earth is reaching out to us for healing, whether you believe you are ready or not. How do you know when you are called? Certainly, it is different for everyone. You could be fortunate to be told outright - via intuition, visions, or voices - that your services are required. For me, however, I spent close to six months experiencing a strange fluttering of the heart, a vibration in my chest that resembled profound anxiety. Eventually, I consulted an energetic healer who described that "spiritual glass ceiling" and declared it was caused by recently accessed heart energy that now needed to be projected... through service.

What is "Service"?

Simply put, service is the practice of giving your time, expertise, or resources to relieve the suffering of others without expecting anything in return. Does this mean that we won't be compensated by those we serve? No. When in service, compensation will show itself in many forms... gifts of love, money, food, shelter. Abundance is available to those in service while Source sees to it that you will have everything you need.

Whenever reward is *expected*, two things occur. 1) We interfere with the natural OUTWARD flow of energies from a spiritually secure heart; 2) We tell the universe that we do not trust Source to give us what we need.

The Kabbalah distills the difference between the unawakened man and God down to essentially one thing: Man is primarily concerned about *getting*; God is wholly concerned with *giving*. According to the Zohar, as we learn to give more altruistically we move on to higher worlds of less suffering and more freedom. Even though we can evolve into these higher levels we still can maintain a footprint in the lower worlds where we must continue to serve those who have not yet had our experience of awakening. Our influence in these lower worlds can seem almost magical to those uninitiated into the higher realms. We essentially discover and then prove our power to change reality with our consciousness alone.

Isolation = Weakness   Connection = Power

Cultures of our distant past were in touch with their powers of conscious manifestation because of their social commitment to the idea of interconnectedness. An example that comes to mind is the ancient Maya, where the greeting *"In Lak'ech"* originated, which means *"I am another you"*. The Mayan are the same "primitive" people who engineered massive pyramids and created a cosmic calender system which has precisely predicted every step of humanity's conscious evolution.

Our current Western culture, however, is plagued with a severe sense of isolation fueled by our capitalistic system of commerce, where everything has a price... even you! For a capitalistic system to survive, it requires all of us to be addicted to consumption. The more we consume, the more we buy. The more we buy, the more our economy supposedly prospers. For us to consume so obsessively, we must also buy into this core belief that we are absolutely isolated from each other. This isolation is perpetuated by a system that instigates competition on every level. Such pervasive cultural competition to consume is what ultimately sets us against each other.

When we believe that we are isolated, it makes no difference that our next-door neighbor drives to the same area where you both work every day. We simply "know" we need to buy our own car. In fact, in America, we are so isolated within our own families to think every member over the age of 16 *deserves* their very own car. Of course, the automobile is just the most obvious example of that plenitude of products we must possess in order to define our own isolated individuality - regardless of the obvious intelligence in sharing those products with those around us.

It should be no secret to you now how the seductive, destructive voices of mainstream media are championed by those who profit most from capitalism. More than ever it remains in their self-serving interest to fan the flames of our isolation by making us fear each other through the systemic manipulation of negative news which deliberately keeps us woefully un-informed. Mainstream media keeps us jealous of one another with a ceaseless bombardment of unnatural representations of Beauty and Success. Finally, Big Media warps our values by offering disposable Bliss on credit so we, too, can enjoy the lifestyles of the rich and famous.

You can turn off all media in your own life, but we still live in a media-manipulated reality. The resulting isolation has made us so insecure in our own bodies and so frantically desperate in our minds and so impoverished in our spirits that we are driven to commit nasty acts of greed and selfishness upon each other every day, rationalizing our guilt and deceptions with that cruelest of cultural catch phrases: *"nothing personal...it's just business"*.

The Science and Practice of Manifesting Unity Consciousness

So here we dwell at the height of western *civilization*, with all its alleged comforts and convenient technologies. Yet our planet is showing all the signs of sickness from a virus we cynically call *humanity*. If our bodies were to harbor such a rapidly multiplying, all-consuming virus we would certainly die in a matter of days. Mother Earth is far more resilient and is revealing to those who will listen that we are *not* alone, that we can all tap into a power far greater than anything we imagined. The only catch is that this power must be used for healing.

For true healing to happen there must be a conscious and sustained connection between the healer and what is sick, whether it be your fellow man or some other facet of Mother Earth. Service to others is the most rapid and rewarding path to that connection.

I guess I've driven the point home that the true power of creation lies in connection. Every sort of connective creation always has a healing component and the connection is not just between healer and what is sick. There is an even stronger creative power given to those who *come together* for the higher goal of healing. The ultimate purpose of this book is to explore ways to understand and *collectively* channel the energies of healers to produce a manifesting force that is powerful enough to deal with a planetary crisis that seems beyond our abilities to fix with current technology or through the efforts of spiritually-guided healers who act in isolation.

The secret behind "The Secret"

Like the shallow prayers of conventional religion, much of the recent New Age exploration into manifestation and creative visualization - popularized in *The Secret* - are mere extensions of that same isolated, individualized mind-set rooted in self-centered consumption. *I want to manifest a new car. I will create that house I've al-*

ways wanted, I will get that promotion that I deserve. In the vast arena of creation, these are very small potatoes. Thus your access to truly creative power is equally small and limited.

The power of prayer is not an asking for things. Many adherents of this alleged *Secret* have voiced frustration, felt more inadequate, even experienced guilt when they cannot reliably nor conveniently manifest what they desire. This is because their desires are not originating from their hearts. And it is your heart which is the nuclear power plant that energizes the authentic creation process.

In the next chapter we will explore how vastly powerful your heart is compared to your mind. We will also explore how what you think you want changes for the better when you let your desires arise straight from your heart.

In conclusion, it is through selfless service to others that we access this creative power of the heart. And it is only through the heart that we can be both powerful transformers and powerfully transformed. And it is through acting *in unison* as creators that we will manifest new realities with the power and wisdom necessary to deal with the crisis we currently face.

Exercises for Chapter 1

1. Identify items belonging to you that have a strong spiritual connection and meaning. These objects can be anything from spiritual texts, pictures of loved ones, or the comb your grandmother gave you before she passed away. Take these items and arrange them thoughtfully in a place in your residence that is sacred and filled with positive energy. This will be your altar, your sacred place of meditation.

It is important that you feel secure in this place, so if you live with a person who would not respect your altar, it is vital that you keep the altar somewhere safe, like your room. Never allow your altar to be trashed or neglected. If you are fortunate to be on a spiritual path with someone who lives with you, it will benefit your relationship greatly to share a common combined altar in the house.

Understand that the altar is a representation of your divine presence. It is absolutely appropriate that this altar evolve with you, to be added to or subtracted from at anytime and change as you change.

2. During meditation, think of something you've encountered in your day-to-day life that broke your heart. It could be the desperate-looking man at the intersection asking to work for food. It could be a school in your area that is struggling to educate its students. It could be someone in your book club who struggles with depression. In short, seek out very personal sources of sadness. Whatever you encounter in your day to day life that breaks your heart should be where you offer yourself in service. It is important that you focus on what breaks your heart within your local context. It is too easy to focus on large-scale catastrophes across the globe. Such long distance sympathy keeps us disassociated from both the suffering and our role in the suffering. (It is also most produc-

tive to serve those you know, above and beyond any "random acts of kindness" you may choose to provide among strangers.) If you are having trouble determining exactly how you can serve try the following meditation:

Bring yourself to stillness, noticing the natural rhythm of your breath. Relax into your body. Meditate upon what breaks your heart. Try to truly feel the bitter-sweet pain of the heart-break. Pretend that you are lowering yourself by rope into a dark cavern. As you get closer to the bottom of the cavern you see a lantern on the floor illuminating a letter sealed in wax. Break the seal, open the letter, and read how you can serve.[1]

Now that you've identified your calling for service find others with a similar calling and collaborate in your efforts to serve.

---

1. Adapted from Andrew Harvey - http://instituteforsacredactivism.org

Accessing the Power of the Heart

One of the most difficult journeys I have made is the one leading to my own heart. As an adopted child in an abusive family I learned early on to shield my heart behind a labyrinth of defenses to protect my most vulnerable and valuable asset. However, I struggled through life long after I had escaped that abuse. I struggled because the path to my own heart had become a dark maze, full of clever trap doors and land mines so even I could no longer find my own center.

Like so many others I dispassionately dragged my way through existence, always seeking "something" yet unconsciously sabotaging the very thing I was seeking... true connection. I set myself up for frustration after frustration, never understanding the nature of my isolated suffering.

Somewhere along what seemed my aimless path I was fortunate to stumble upon grace. In my late thirties, kundalini released from the base of my spine, setting fire to the established illusions that were the boundaries and battlements separating me from others. The vectors of my life were forever altered, as each new day felt like another step toward some deeper connection. One day I found that connection with one special heart, then another, then others, until, ultimately, my path was cleared and led directly to the all-encompassing heart of God. The Source.

Your heart is the nexus of connection with everything else. All of us are constantly seeking this deep connection whether we care to admit it or not. It is a basic instinct woven into the very fabric of our DNA. It is one of the most powerful drives in the whole spectrum of human desires. The heart connection is an ultimate magnetic force of Togetherness that brings us back into Oneness which is the direct experience of God.

When we contemplate The Power of the Heart, most of us think in terms of Love. Cynics and scientists have suggested that love is simply a complex electromagnetic biochemical phenomenon in the brain. However, in the fullness of time, countless documented experiences insist Love is a far more pervasive force that can feel and heal over long distances instantaneously! Are these conflicting beliefs? Or do both positions view the same truth from different perspectives? Draw your own conclusions after understanding what those rigorous scientific studies have concluded about your heart.

Science of the heart

Before 1991, it was the common understanding among medical professionals that the heart was simply an efficient muscle that pumped blood throughout the body. Yet, we have always credited the heart as being the seat of great emotion, namely love.

Dr. J. Andrew Armour shattered the limited paradigms of medicine and gave scientific credence to what we thought we knew all along about the emotional heart.

It was Dr. Armour who first discovered an intricate

network of neurons within and surrounding the heart which essentially elevated this muscle to the status of a "little brain." This revelation led to further discoveries that offer us these factual insights into the awesome power of this organ.

Heart facts

The heart's very intricate network of neurons allows it to act independently from the cranial brain. It can take cues from the brain and vice versa. But these two organs can also act completely independent of each other. Your heart does everything the cranial brain does - think, remember, sense, feel. Such independence allows for the success of heart transplants.

- In the fetus, the heart-brain is developed long before the cranial brain. As a consequence, our emotional nature is developed before our logical nature, which keeps us more primally connected to our powerful unconscious.
- The heart's electrical field is about 60 times greater in amplitude than the electrical activity generated by the brain.[1]
- The heart has an intricate network comprised of precisely the same neurons, neurotransmitters, proteins, and support cells found within the brain.
- Dr. Armour describes the brain and nervous system as "a distributed parallel processing system consisting of separate but interacting groups of neuronal processing centers distributed throughout the body."[2]
- The human heart generates a magnetic field that is 5000 times more powerful than the brain. This field extends far beyond the physical heart. Beyond the concept of your "aura", some research suggests that this heart-field can extend in the magnitude of miles.
- Current data from the Global Coherence Initiative suggests that the collective power of many humans sharing

the same emotion can affect the Earth's magnetic field. This poses massive implications for planetary healing.[4]

Your heart as the great communicator
The human heart is our organ of connection in both the physical and energetic realm.

- *Electromagnetically* - The heart creates a powerful electromagnetic field that communicates with our entire body as well as with our external environment - perhaps for miles.
- *Rhythmically* - our heart responds to our emotional states with its rhythm of beat. It is well documented how yogis can purposefully manipulate their own heart's rhythms to dramatically alter their physiological and emotional state.
- *Neurologically* - The cranial brain receives messages through nerve impulses that are intimately connected to the beating of your heart.
- *Biochemically* - the heart is also medically categorized as an endocrine gland which produces its own hormones and neurotransmitters separate from brain chemistry.

All of the heart's abilities to connect and communicate pale in comparison to what happens when the heart achieves what is called a state of coherence.

Coherence - The healing song of the heart

The heart has 7 distinct muscle groups that produce different vibrational patterns. One can see these patterns in relationship to each other on an EKG chart. Usually these patterns are out of sync and jumbled. Yet when the heart is in a non-judgmental or love state, the 7 muscle groups take on the same rhythm. This coherence of rhythm builds on itself, and consequently amplifies the frequency.

As shown in figure 2-1, the EKG chart of a heart in a coherent love rhythm, has frequency peaks that follow the *phi ratio*. The phi ratio is approximately 1.618, which is gradually reached when dividing a number in the Fibonacci by its preceding number. The Fibonacci sequence (1, 1, 2, 3, 5, 8, 13, ...) is created by simply adding a number in the sequence to the preceding number. This sequence is pervasive throughout nature and can be considered a universal constant.

Frequencies nested as a phi ratio creates an efficient path or harmonic channel for communication. Some data suggests an even higher dimensional communication potential. Frequencies closely following the phi ratio can accommodate the nesting of higher informational vibrations. The phi ratio allows for frequencies to change harmonic scales without losing any energy or information. This allows for a high degree of communication within your body and to the world outside.

Figure 2-1, EKG of coherent heart

Internal coherency acts as an entrainment wave that invites incoherent and stressed electromagnetic (EM) fields to move into harmony with the more coherent EM field. This phenomenon is the same thing that happens in a shop full of pendulum clocks. Regardless of what rhythm the individual clocks started out with, over a period of time all of the pendulums will begin to swing in unison. The same phenomenon is present in a house of close-knit ladies who eventually find their menstruation happening at the same time of the month.

Since a coherent heart produces vibrational patterns that are stronger than any other part of the body, it can entrain the rest of the body - especially your brain. This can also extend to the reality beyond your skin. Have you noticed what happens to people in a room when you are truly in your heart?

When the heart is in coherence there are many advantages to your body:

- Less stress
- Cortisol and DHEA (a hormone that decreases in the body with age) are both made from the same chemical precursor. When the body is stressed, that precursor is depleted to make cortisol, so less is available to make the more beneficial DHEA.
- When the heart is in coherence, encouraging messages are sent to prompt the cells of your body to replicate.
- The thymus gland sits above the heart, primarily tasked to produce hormones that protect the cells of the body and improve immunity. A coherent heart increases the thymus' ability to produce these hormones. The thymus gland in children is large in comparison to its size in adults. In most adults the thymus is practically atrophied. What does that say about our ability to maintain loving states as we become adults?[5]

The importance of gratitude to maintain coherence

A very powerful way of maintaining a state of heart coherence is to be grateful for everything you have, and every drop of vitality you have to enjoy it with. Make it a conscious priority to be thankful. Make a mental list of your blessings on a constant basis throughout your day. Write it on your arm to remind yourself, for God's sake. After a while it will become more second nature.

At some point you will question some dark, dire

thoughts which inevitably arise from your tireless ego, an ego which is designed to repeatedly insist you are alone and separate from the rest of the universe. Being in gratitude reminds you that you are indeed a part of it all.

Manifesting from the heart always results in healing

Healing is the restoration of balance in an organism or system. To those in the energetic arts, the area of the heart represents the Anahata chakra that both integrates and unifies. That is why love is regarded as the ultimate force of healing. Yogis consider the heart to be the place of perfect balance between Heaven and Earth, physical body and spiritual body

When we open the heart chakra we always make the realization of connection, that we are all one. This connection is compassionate and non-judgmental. As Bodhisattvas, we will not cross over into enlightenment unless and until we can bring others along via the process of healing.

Remember - whenever we heal, we cannot impose our own sense of balance. As compassionate practitioners, we must act non-judgmentally as a catalyst for who and what is being healed, to create their own sense of balance.

This sense of balance is negated when we follow current, popular manifestation strategies that utilize only our minds. Every brain has two hemispheres. Whenever we create from the head we use a known instrument of polarity, thus whatever our minds create will be - by definition and functionality - dualistic.

No matter how intense our intent is to create good, the most logical and balanced mind inevitably creates both good and bad. However, your heart knows only unity and can create only unity. So the dark side of this dichotomy is never present in what is crafted in your heart. The result is always a healing effect.

Mind based logic vs Heart based feeling

Imagination. Abstraction. Evaluation. Insight. Common sense. Whatever the mind creates requires logic. And everything it creates will follow a logical trail from one state to the next. Nevertheless, the mind's creative process is always a miracle of evolution to behold. But, regardless of our intelligence, education, wisdom, or experiences, the creation of that miracle is constrained by the limits of our logic. It is indeed true when people of deep faith say that everything is a miracle. The miracle of heart creation, however, is not bound by a dualistic or logical paradigm, but rather liberated by pure, simple feelings. Imagine healing without having to go through all the logical, medical steps of analysis, treatment, and rehabilitation.

Witness consciousness

If there is one lesson that can be distilled from this book, it's that to truly improve upon reality you must manifest from the heart... a coherent heart, to be specific. However, before any of us can reach that blissful state of coherence we must all energetically access our hearts. In yogic terms this means becoming sensitive to the energies and messages from the Anahata, or the heart chakra.

Fully accessing the heart may not be easy for some. For me it was one of the biggest and most rewarding challenges of my life. Because of childhood abuse, I experienced betrayal, humiliation, and abandonment during the time my heart was developmentally ripe for bonding.

It was a sweetly painful ordeal accessing my heart. When I dared to allow myself the experience of true connection to others the first thing I felt in those recesses of my heart was mostly pain because that was the only experience my heart knew how to reference. To this day, whenever I encounter unexplored depths of my heart, my first reaction is often a baptism of tears to clear away that familiar vibration of pain. Only then is that empty space filled with the much higher vibration of love and connection.

The pain I experienced would be far from "sweet" if I had not developed what is called a *witness consciousness* or a distance between the emotions and the observer of the emotions. I was fortunate to experience this rather rapidly when I was taught the first level Cosmic Cobra breath by one of my beloved gurus, Sunyata Saraswati. This extremely powerful breath opened my intuitive third eye and gave me the distance required to witness my emotions. Without my training in both tantra and other energetic forms of yoga, it would have been difficult to safely experience the physical release of a multitude of painful emotions which wracked my body.

How do we develop this witness consciousness if you are not practicing the Cosmic Cobra breath? It can be achieved by first having the intellectual understanding that we are not our emotions, and that emotions are simply bodily responses to what's going on in our minds. We do, indeed, have powerful and doubtful thoughts which refuse to be silent. But you need not give them authority to make that leap to the physical realm and take control over your body.

The second step to achieve a witness consciousness is to meditate on a daily basis. It is most effective to meditate in the morning, when we awaken, and in the evening, before we go to sleep. Even a few short minutes of silence can provide great benefits, providing you first quiet your chatterbox brain long enough to find that essential focus to calmly, quietly, and comfortably examine your emotions as they emerge.

When many hearts beat as one

Connecting at the level of the heart always requires an element of surrender. This is true whether that connection is between two hearts or 7 billion. This deep rooted urge to connect is not just a human trait, it is cosmic phenomenon. It is the built-in essence of the universal plan to push consciousness towards higher states of complexity, love, and awareness, ultimately leading toward the awareness of its own divine power as a creator.

These higher states of awareness or consciousness usually occur in spurts. The visionary Ray Kurzweil calls them *singularities*. A singularity is that point in the evolution of any system where the elements of that system create something entirely new and highly evolved. This new entity is beyond any explanations within the old system. The sum inevitably becomes greater than its parts

In our case, it means that we are rapidly approaching a point where a new, higher consciousness will be created from the foundations provided by humanity's current state of consciousness. Yet this higher state cannot be adequately explained within the paradigm of our current cultural awareness.

Several singularities have happened at regular intervals in the 4.6 billion years of Mother Earth's own conscious evolution. Historically, each singularity involved states of consciousness surrendering to a more complex, more evolved consciousness. Ever since our Big Bang birth, atoms came together to form molecules, molecules group into proteins, proteins form DNA, DNA forms unicellular organisms, cells join together to form animals and plants, then within the plant and animal kingdoms there have been many leaps forward in consciousness. Take note that each preceding level of consciousness continues to exist, but surrenders to something on a grander scale.

Timing is everything. It is absolutely critical right now that those of us - and those we love - who have walled off our hearts must begin to break down those walls with some sense of urgency. Breakthroughs that took years in the old sense of time can now happen in moments because of the accelerated speed of creation. For further scientific study, you might google "quantum physics" + "accelerated time" and you will learn that cutting-edge physicists agree - time really is moving faster today!

So here we stand, evolution's own Homo Sapien Sapien, now being called upon to surrender to something bigger than our individual selves. By voluntarily surrendering to this state of collective coherence we can also more gracefully ease into what inevitably awaits us as a higher, more evolved consciousness.

For those who choose to stay around to witness and participate in this transformation, your surrender and the resulting connection will all happen in the same place... your heart.

References

1. http://www.healingheartpower.com/power-heart.html

2. http://www.heartmath.org/research/science-of-the-heart.html

3. caltek.net/.../physicsofphi/PhysicsofPHI.html

4. Bradden, G. (2009). Fractal time: The secret of 2012 and a new world age. Carlsbad, CA. Hay House, Inc.

5. Avinasha, B. (2003). The Ipsalu formula: A method for tantra bliss. Valley Village, CA. Ipsalu Publishing.

Exercises for Chapter 2

1. Kalipatra - The Wishing Tree Meditation

Below the heart chakra is a small lotus with eight petals called the Anandakanda Lotus. Inside this lotus is a celestial wishing tree from the Heaven of Indra- the Kalpataru. In front of this tree is a bejeweled altar which is believed to hold the most sincere desires of the heart. These desires are not usually what our mind desires, but rather the deeper yearnings of our soul. When we wish upon this tree with deep earnestness, our wishes become liberated. In fact, the Kalpataru gives us even more than we originally preferred, which results in freedom (moksa).

First lie down comfortably. It is advised to take a few minutes to anchor oneself, focus, and relax the muscles. Only do this exercise in an environment that feels safe and comfortable.

Breathe deeply- in and out - and repeat this breath in a circular motion by filling your lungs, heart, and then belly... Hold... release the air in your belly, heart, and lungs. Slowly become alert to the heartbeat and listen to its pulse. Envision the heart pumping blood throughout the body by the elaborate network of arteries and veins. Then visualize each of the circulatory pathways above the heart as branches of a tree. Visualize those circulatory pathways below the heart as roots to the tree, pulsing with the life and energy of your blood. Be mindful of the oxygen as it is pumped out through the heart, out through the chest, the shoulders, down the arms, into the hands, and back again. This must be followed again down the belly, the legs, knees, and feet, and back up again through the body, and home, to the heart. Every drop of blood that goes through the heart returns to be rejuvenated again with breath, air, and life.

Think of the heart as a sacred tree. Its branches are a web of life stretching all through the body, and then out into the world. The trunk of the tree is our core, our being, and our vital self. The very foundation of the tree, the roots, also spread out from the bottom of this core into Mother Earth finding food and water that supports and gives substance. From the top of our core are the branches, their leaves, and desires of the heart. They gather together the sun and wind that energize our desires. These desires flower and fruit and fall upon the ground to grow again.

In front of this tree is an altar decked out in jewels. We can make an offering to this altar- either something we are willing to giving up, like a bad habit - or something we would like to give to ourselves, like healing, creativity, or the devotion to practice. This offering is an exchange for the granting of our wish.

Next, breathe into the heart and feel the pain and the bliss. Dig deep to actually feel the most vulnerable longings of your heart. It is not important for us to put a name on anything, just FEEL it. Breath into these feelings, allowing them to flow through the whole body, pulsating outward, returning, and pulsating outward again. Let the deepest of your longings fill the branches of the tree.

When the tree is saturated with the deepest cravings of the heart, envision that a single white dove flies to the centre of the tree, sits on a branch, tilts its head to one side, cocks it to the other, and listens deeply to the desires that have been expressed. Connect deeply in spiritual union with this bird. Allow the bird to come close to the heart and let the heart (not the mind) speak its deepest longing to the bird. It's OK if specific images come to mind, but do not search for them. Let this process be completely organic and just watch the desires surface on their own momentum. When we feel a sense of completeness it is time to kiss the bird goodbye and watch it fly away to the heavens to perform its work. Just let the bird go and forget about your wish. Trust that the bird will carry the wishes to the powers that be, so that they may be satisfied in the best way feasible for all concerned.

2. Exploring the Heart - Sacred Space Meditation

The first part of the mediation is called the Unity Breath. This breath is important because it unifies the loving presence of the Cosmic Father and Mother Earth in the heart, which allows you to tangibly become the beloved Cosmic Child, completing the Holy Trinity, one of the deepest archetypes of the Collective Unconscious.

Imagine your most beloved place in nature. Feel the loving and nourishing presence of Mother Earth. Imagine the smell of rich soil, feel the caressing breezes across your face. Feel completely at one with your surroundings. Feel nothing but pure love for Mother Earth and let this feeling flow throughout your entire body.

Feel the presence of someone who represents a nurturing mother figure in your life. It is fine if it is not the mother who raised you. Feel the caring, unbounded love that only a mother can have for a child.

When you are completely filled with maternal loving bliss, allow this love to coalesce in your heart as a golden glowing sphere of light. Release this light and let it travel down your spine into the ground and then deep into the Earth. Just wait patiently for this love to be returned to you... It will come if your love for Mother Earth was indeed sincere.

When the love of Mother Earth comes to you, just allow your self to feel the love. Do not try to direct it in anyway. This is an exercise in surrendering... Just FEEL.

When you are ready, begin to focus on the sky. Imagine the vastness of the heavens, the Sun, the planets, the Milky Way, other galaxies, and the entire universe. Feel the wise, loving presence of Father Sky.

Feel the presence of a nurturing father figure in your life. Feel the unconditional love, the wise hand of guidance and protection. Know that you will want for nothing. Your father will provide everything.

When you are ready allow this love for the paternal to coalesce in the heart as a golden, glowing sphere of light. When you are ready, release this light and allow it to travel up your spine from your heart and out deep into the heavens. Wait patiently for Father Sky to return this love to you. You are now a part of the cosmic, holy trinity of mother, father, and child. Bask in this sacred moment. Feel the presence of God pervasive in everything.

The second part of this meditation is finding your way into the heart. There is a male path which visualizes the whirling vortex of energy that envelopes the heart. There is also a female path that relies more upon intuition. It doesn't matter which path you choose whether you are male or female.

Imagine your consciousness inside your skull. Feel what it is like inside the confines of that space, with the dome of hard bone surrounding you.

Then move your consciousness down into your throat and feel the softness of the flesh, the fragile structure of your windpipe. Visualize yourself as your consciousness standing on a diving platform, the kind that is very high like you would see in the in the Olympics.

When you are ready, jump from the platform and fall into a flowing whirlpool that is the toroidal field of energy flowing into your heart as shown on the following page.

Your heart's toroidal field is either spinning clockwise or counter clockwise. Just pay attention to how you feel and you will know which direction. Let yourself, as your consciousness, fall into the whirlpool of energy, like a leaf falling into a swirling water spout. Imagine spinning faster and faster as you get closer to the center of the spout. Imagine yourself falling and falling until you are in complete stillness.

Figure 2-2 Heart's Toroidal Field

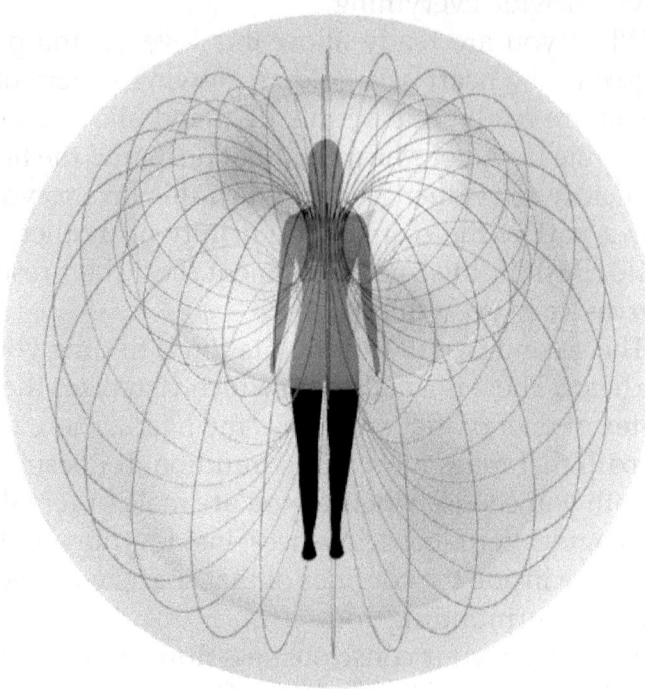

If you prefer the female path just imagine your consciousness in your throat passing through the membrane of your heart into its dark depths.

Look around. Chances are it is dark and warm. If it is, then command that there be light.

You may hear a vibration. This is the sound that permeates your heart space. Listen for a while. When you are ready begin to softly hum this vibration. Try to duplicate the sound as closely as possible. Just keep humming.

Look around your heart space for a faint green glow. Follow that glow until you come to a large trunk. Open this trunk and you will see a large, brilliant, glowing, deep green emerald. This is the very sacred place of your heart. Imagine yourself merging with the emerald that is radiating the beautiful green light of the sacred space of your heart. Stop humming and remain very quiet. You will probably hear a higher pitched vibration here. Try to softly duplicate this vibration with a hum. Remember the pitch of this hum. It is your way to directly get back to this place anytime you wish.

Abundance addendum to this meditation

If you care to go further with this particular meditation and internalize even more overflowing abundance, you can follow along through this next optional section.

- As you are continue to hum the vibration of your heart's sacred space, imagine the most beautiful, pristine lake in the world on an absolutely perfect Fall or Spring day.
- Imagine a child picking up an emerald that embodies the sacred space of your heart. Visualize that child throwing the emerald far out into the middle of this deep, tranquil lake. Allow your consciousness to follow - flying, falling, dropping down deep to the bottom of the lake. Feel your heart's vibrant green light illuminating the watery depths.
- Now picture thousands of people surrounding the lake. Every person carries empty bottles, pots, or jugs. See them bending down to gather water to drink. This water is infused and enriched with the emerald light from your Heart's most sacred love.
- An underground spring will replenish you with an infinite supply regardless of how many drink from your lake. The Love in your Heart will never run dry. This represents the true nature of your abundance.

3. Emanating Heart Cobra Breath

This kriya-type meditation is wonderful for both opening your heart and deeply connecting to others in your life. The meditation begins with creating a list of 10 people in your life who possess the greatest charge for you. This charge can have an overwhelming positive or negative effect. Go through this list and direct the energy created from this exercise to each person on your list.

1. Sit in meditative pose.
2. Imagine the infinite wisdom and unconditional love of Father Sky. Picture the vastness of the heavens as you contemplate the nurturing, protective love given to you by a true Father Figure in your life.
3. As you inhale, bring the tip of your tongue to the roof of your mouth or back of your throat, whichever channels the most energy. Imagine the golden light of Father Sky being pulled into your crown. As this energy is pulled into your body, internalize the *earliest* name you gave to your father (*Daddy, Papa, Da-Da*) to establish that connection with your Inner Child.
4. While you are doing all of this, close your Mūla Bandha or Root half-way. For women, your root is activated by squeezing the cervix and vaginal muscles behind the cervix where the uterus projects into the vagina (popularly know among women as *kegel* exercises. For men, your root is activated by squeezing the perineal muscles between anus and scrotum.
5. Continue to inhale the golden energy from Father Sky, entering through your crown and now collecting in your heart. See your heart glowing with this golden energy.
6. During the second half of your inhale, squeeze the remaining half of your root and imagine pulling the golden love energy of Mother Earth up into your root, up your

spine, and collecting in your heart. As you pull Her energy upwards, internalize the earliest name you gave to your mother (Ma, Ma Ma, Mommy).
7. Slowly release your Root and voice the mantra AH while mentally projecting the golden/green energy of your heart to the heart of some you love. It is best to visualize looking in the eyes of this person while you project. After you have felt the heart connection of a loved one, the rest of your practice should be focused on people that you don't have an open heart toward.

3

The Mechanics of Intention

> *"It's the biological creature that fashions the stories, that makes the observations, and that gives names to things. And therein lies the great expanse of our oversight that, until now, science hasn't confronted the one thing that's at once most familiar and most mysterious - consciousness."*
> **Robert Lanza, MD**

Introduction

One historical trend that you can depend on is that, eventually, every major scientific revelation exposing the nature of reality profoundly changes society's understanding of what is possible. Take, for instance, the civilized mind-set before 1600 AD. The mainstream public *knew* the Earth was the center of the universe; a view espoused by Ptolemy and endorsed by the Catholic church. Thanks to Copernicus, however, an entire civilization came to reject the old beliefs and accept the evidence that their Earth orbits the sun like all the other planets in our solar system. Once we were no longer the center of the Universe, a radical change in thinking opened the door into a deeper, more realistic understanding of where we stood in the blueprint of the Cosmos.

A century later, Newton gave us the Laws of Motion and the theory of gravity. As a consequence, our new reality embraced a predictable understanding of everything from the motion of the planets for navigation, to the precise force needed from a steam engine to run textile looms during the industrial revolution. Fundamental physics became another undeniable *Truth* which compelled humanity to master their world with raw power and mighty machines. We did so because we saw we could.

Our mastery of the physical realm was extended even further when Einstein theorized that Man's influence over space and time was limited to the speed of light, because Einstein proved nothing could go faster than the speed of light... until the 1930's, when quantum physicists revealed the vast realm inside every atom. To explain this newest layer of Reality, these western scientific visionaries spoke like Eastern gurus to describe the nature of *Nature* in the following ways:

- Matter is directly influenced by consciousness.
- Particles that have made contact once continue to act in concert with each other even when separated over unfathomable distances.
- Our bodies are emitters of the most coherent, powerful light found in nature.
- Our DNA is an extremely efficient transmitter and receiver of information in both this dimension and beyond.

Imagine what our lives will look like when the revelations proven by quantum physics become accepted Truth within the mainstream belief system!

There is a catch, however, to how *far* science can expand our ideas of what's possible... or, rather, how *fast*. Change, itself, is always instantaneous. Yet it can take years, decades, even centuries before any bold paradigm shifts the main-stream of public consciousness. In fact, the adoption of a new way of explaining the world is only embraced when the paradigms of the old world have reached their limits of explanation.

We've now reached our limits of understanding Reality through the lenses of Newton's classical physics and Einstein's theory of relativity. As a social species, we are slowly realizing how our *power* wielded by machines that burn crude forms of energy has ultimately brought us to a place of *powerlessness*.

When Science has explored the boundaries and paved our way with knowledge, we will act on the simple, inescapable truth that our planet can no longer sustain unbridled consumption with profound disregard for balance. Today, laymens' books and movies popularize quantum physics, bringing us insight into an untapped "scientific", God-given, faith-building, alternative power source... the power of consciousness.

This chapter provides a very brief overview of the scientific viewpoints regarding consciousness and intent upon the physical realm. Moreover, this chapter outlines what's required for intent to be effective.

If you are not particularly science-driven in your beliefs, it is perfectly OK to skip the beginning of this chapter and resume reading from *Criteria for Heart Based Healing*.

Nonlocality

Picture yourself in the 1920's. Imagine the look on Neils Bohr's face the day he realized - after countless checks of his equations - that whenever connected atomic particles are separated, *they are still directly affected by what happens to the other*, kind of like that Cheech and Chong movie about the Corsican Twins. If one brother got cut by a sword the other brother bled.

This is no longer theory, but experimentally proven. Once regarded as *sympathetic magic,* today it is a natural law in the sub-atomic universe. Bohr referred to this accepted phenomenon as *quantum entanglement* or *nonlocality*. Yet matter does not have to be as small as quantum particles to experience nonlocality.

Molecules are the basis of chemistry and chemistry is the basis of all matter and life. Tom Rosenbaum at the James Franck Institute found that a grain of one type of salt also conforms to these laws of nonlocality. This single grain contains thousands of atoms bound as molecules. Thus we discover how complex molecules of tangible matter also obey the spooky laws of quantum physics. Essentially, we are infused with enough power to influence the rest of existence through an intricate web of quantum entanglement.

In short, cutting-edge science proves (and continues to prove): WE ARE ALL ONE! Those of us on the path *know* this. But for science to declare it as a *Fact* means society as a whole has begun to shift toward that *knowing* as well.

Accepting non-locality means accepting the earth-shattering reality that we each can influence anything without the limiting factors of time and space. And there is more math to prove that our doing this together creates compound dividends. *If this is hitting you for the first time, it is perfectly OK to let out a...* WOW. The implications for *intention* are gigantic.

The Observer always affects the observed

Subatomic particles exist in a state of infinite potential until influenced by conscious acts of observation. This was proven in Young's slit experiment.

This experiment was originally designed to decide whether light was a particle or a wave. Shooting light photons through one slit, as shown below, would produce a simple verticle band resembling the slit with the light growing dimmer as it radiates outward from the center. - this speaks to the PARTICLE nature of light.

Figure 3-1 Slit experiment with one slit, expressing the particle nature of light [1]

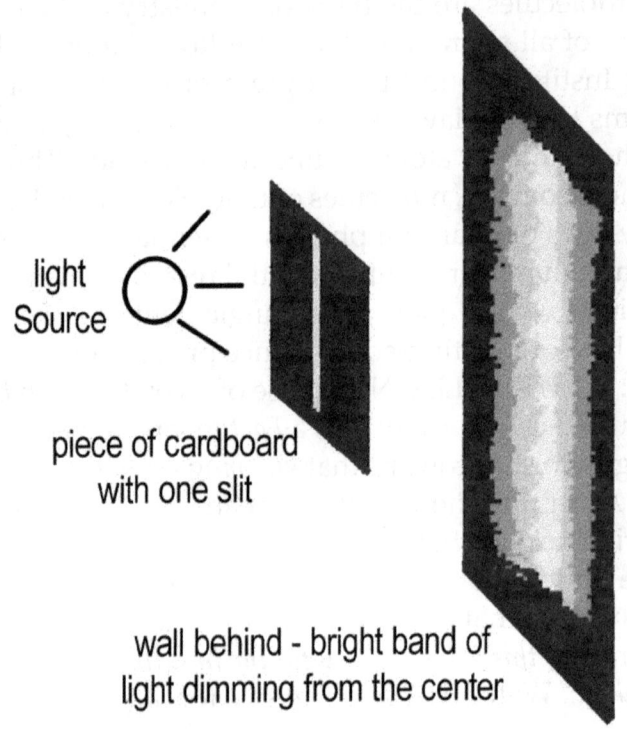

However, when light photons are shot through two vertical slits, an interference pattern of bands of darkness and light becomes evident. This clearly speaks to the wave nature of light, as shown below.

Figure 3-2   Slit experiment with two slits expressing the wave nature of light [1]

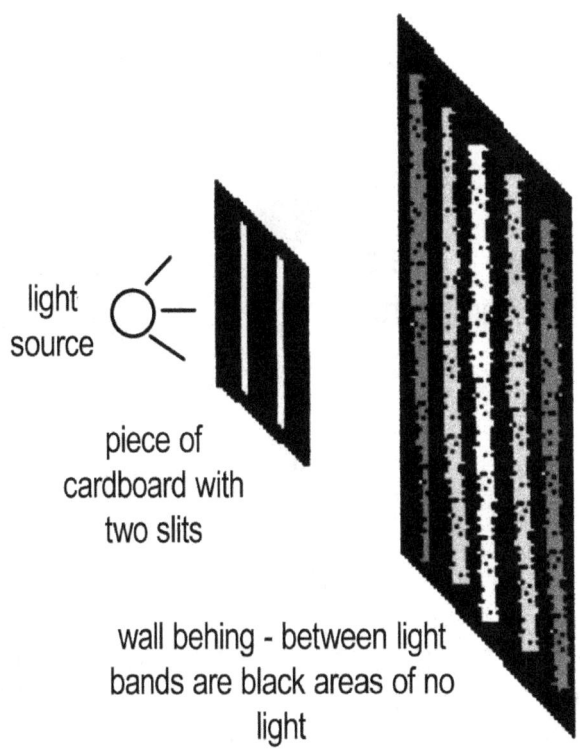

light source

piece of cardboard with two slits

wall behing - between light bands are black areas of no light

   Yet when a detector is set up to see which photons are going through what slit... the wave function of light collapses to a solid place in time and space to act as particles producing two simple vertical bands of light dimming as it radiates from the center.

Figure 3-3 Slit experiment with two slits expressing the wave nature of light [1]

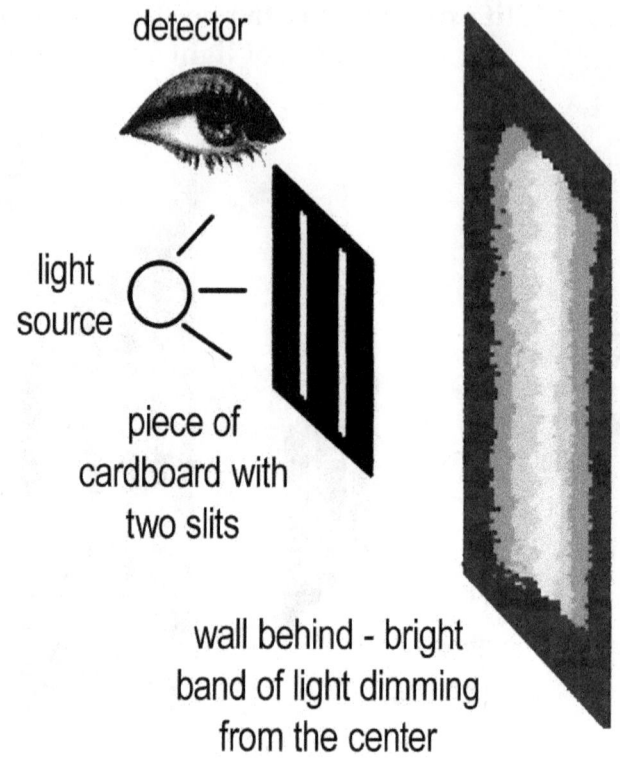

So, if a wave is *Energy* and a particle is *Matter*, how can light be both? The simple action of observation collapses the wave function that has no definite position. What was once a wave becomes a particle possessing one specific measurable position in time and space. [2]

Biophotonic coherence - We are all light

In the previous chapter, we discussed how the muscles of the heart can beat together in love and create a harmonic, coherent set of frequencies that nest in each other to amplify their resonant strength. *Particles making waves...so to speak.*

This can happen with coherent light, too. Fritz-Alvert Popp found that all living things give off a constant stream of tiny particles of light or photons he calls *biophotonic emissions*. He believed it is the channel that communicates within and outside all living things and, moreover, this light orchestrates, or at least choreographs, the core cellular processes of living organisms.

Using a machine called a photomultiplier, Popp was able to count how many photons per square centimeter were emitted from an organism. The sicker the organism, the fewer photons it emitted per square centimeter. This gives credence to the perception of someone dying as *their light going out*.

Subsequent experiments were conducted using supercooled, highly sensitive CCDs, a more advanced version of the image chip used in modern video cameras. This produces awe-inducing, perfect negative pictures of anything from a geranium leaf to a human hand. In fact, Schwartz used the equipment to measure the photonic hands of working healers intending healing. It literally showed brilliant light streaming from the hands of the healers. Whether you label it an "aura" or not, science can photograph the fact that all life contains some glow-in-the-dark energy.

More amazing? That faint light emitted from organisms is the most *coherent* light found in nature. As in the case of the heart, light can act as one very powerful frequency, rather than the discordant frequencies of scattered light that we experience in our everyday world. This phenomenon is referred to as *superradiance*.

All life is composed of these superradiant photons that organize around each other in a highly coherent state, much like a room full of tuning forks all tuned to the same frequency. To give you an idea of the power of coherence, think of the light given off by a normal 60-watt bulb. If all the photons of that bulb were to radiate in coherence the energy density of that 60-watt bulb would be thousands of times more intense than that of the sun!

The human body represents one of the most complex examples of individual cells that all march in step to the same tune because of this superradiant, biophotonic light that communicates with our entire body.

What if each powerful human body could come together with other powerful human bodies and achieve a collective state of coherence? Wouldn't that make for quite a light show? The goal of the Collective Heart Yoga is to utilize powerful, esoteric Indian and Tibetan yogic practices to achieve two goals: 1) bring the individual heart to a powerful place of deep love that results in a state of coherence that both amplifies and focuses the energies of the heart, and 2) then coalesce these coherent hearts into an incredibly powerful state of group coherence. From this state we can heal ourselves along with the planet.

Scientific evidence of healing from a coherent heart

All of the studies below were accomplished with healers who maintained a coherent heart state of unconditional love. Please understand these are just a sampling of many historic and on-going studies exploring the healing power of a coherent heart.

- In 1992, Glen Rein along with healer Leonard Laskow, decreased the number of tumor cells in a petri dish by using specified intention, and the imagery of the cancer cells documented this decrease.
- Laskow was able to produce similar results using imagery, and specified, focused intention while winding and unwinding DNA in a solution.

- British healer Matthew Manning was able to influence the adhesion of tumor cells to collagen by focusing his imagery and intention to only one petri dish in a stack of four, suggesting that intention can be specifically focused.
- In 1993, Rein and McCraty were able to influence the winding and unwinding of DNA from a distance of half a mile, well outside what is considered the boundaries of the heart's electromagnetic field.
- A similar experiment with DNA was conducted by Valerie Sadyrin, who was able to influence a DNA sample in California while he was in Russia.

Such empirical experiments demonstrate that coherent heart energy, in addition to having an electromagnetic component, must also have a non-electromagnetic component that can influence healing over long distances.

How am I supposed to believe DNA can be influenced instantaneously over long distances?

Most of us think of DNA as having a primary structure (the genes) and a secondary structure (the helix). This primary and secondary architecture follows the same phi ratio or Golden Mean equally present in the EKG peaks of a coherent heart

Figure 3-4 (next page) is a cycle of the DNA double helix, showing its golden mean proportion (1 angstrom is one 10-billionth of a meter). The ratio 34:21 is approximately the golden mean proportion. [3]

Modern advances in electron microscopy have revealed that DNA also has a tertiary or third structure that consists of the strand winding itself into a pattern. This pattern is described as *toroidal*. Physicists outside the field of biology believe this toroidal shape acts as an antenna of sorts, to both transmit and receive subtle energy outside the electromagnetic spectrum, possibly etheric or higher-dimensional. (Rattemyer 1981)

Figure 3-4 DNA and the Phi ratio [2]

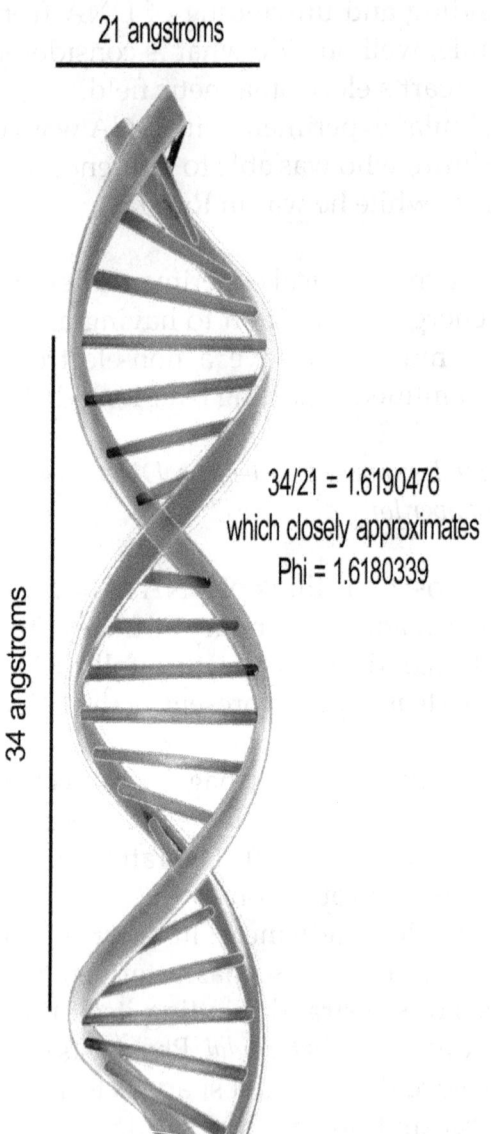

21 angstroms

34/21 = 1.6190476
which closely approximates
Phi = 1.6180339

34 angstroms

Additional evidence for the Toroidal Antenna Model comes from the Russian Academy of Science using a machine called a Laser Correlation Spectroscope. This machine measures the scattering of laser light after it passes through DNA. This machine led to greater understanding of the primary and secondary structure of DNA, and further revealed an energetic third pattern that remains even after the DNA was removed. It is believed that this third, vestigial energetic pattern is the result of DNA's physical toroidal structure. (Poponin 1995).

Criteria for Heart-based healing

Gregg Braden, in the *Isaiah Effect*, outlines what is needed for your heart's intention to manifest. Let's say you want to heal someone from a cancerous tumor in their leg. The following elements are critical for that leg to be healed:

- **Attention** - The first thing that naturally happens is that your attention is brought to that spot where the tumor resides.
- **Intention** - Then make the intention that the leg is completely healthy. Notice my use of the present tense. We shall talk more about that in chapter five.
- **Mental body** - Then you should see in your mind's eye an image of healthy tissue residing where the tumor once existed. This involves the activation of your mental body or mind.
- **Emotional body** - You must engage the emotional body by feeling what it is like having a healthy leg. Note that I'm saying little about the actual tumor because I do not want to put any psychic charge on the actual disease.
- **Physical body** - The final and most forgotten part is the engagement or better yet, *commitment* of the physical body itself toward the act of healing. It could be manifested by

the physical body feeling no pain in the affected leg. Or it could mean the patient making a physical action grounded in the faith that the leg is healed - like walking.

Last thoughts

Influencing the world around us with our thoughts is no longer limited to the domain of mysticism and magic. Science has proven through rigorous experimentation that intention can affect matter, even over long distances.

A world where intentional manifestation is common will happen sooner rather than later. The profound changes we are currently experiencing also prepare us for the day we step up to our true destiny as creative beings of highly coherent light.

However, we must first humbly come together through our hearts, to activate that power. Working models of what is possible will ultimately make tangible the revelations of quantum physics. One day we will all lay down our tools, mothball most machines, and embrace the ultimate technology... Consciousness.

References

1. graphic courtesy of http://www4.ncsu.edu/unity/lockers/users/f/felder/public/kenny/papers/quantum.html

2. Adapted from graphic courtesy of http://www4.ncsu.edu/unity/lockers/users/f/felder/public/kenny/papers/quantum.html

Rein, G. (1996). *Effect of conscious intention on human DNA*, Proceeds of the International Forum on New Science.

Rein G, McCraty R. *Local and non-local effects of coherent heart frequencies on conformational changes in DNA*, Proc. Joint USPA/IAPR Psychotronics Conf., Milwaukee, WI., 1993.

Forgiving Your Self

If you are familiar with the Gnostic Gospels or the more current Course in Miracles², it will be no surprise to you when I say that *forgiveness* is one of the most powerful tools for ending your suffering and ultimately attaining enlightenment.

In addition, true forgiveness is the only path toward clearing away one of the largest impediments to attaining, maintaining, and manifesting from a coherent heart space. The great impediment is guilt. Our guilt is the source of our feelings of not being good enough or not deserving enough. The emotion of guilt shuts down the energetic pathways to all your chakras. For this reason, it is extremely important that we free ourselves from guilt by authentically forgiving ourselves and, by consequence, forgive others.

This chapter will not deal with the most common concept of forgiveness, which is nothing more than a personal decision not to hold the perceived sins of others against them. Such an act is flawed at its core because - as long as we consider an action a sin - it will always resonate with the power of judgment and ultimately separation. Our goal in this book is to identify paths toward connection. True forgiveness allows you to see your fellow man or woman as a mirror that reflects your own nature.

Inside = Outside

One very important concept to translate before any understanding of true forgiveness can begin is the Eastern (Buddhist *and* Hindu) concept of projection. A stretch for many Westerners to grasp, the ancient *and* scientific fact is: Nothing in this world has meaning *except for the meaning we assign*.

Scientists understand how the human brain has evolved biologically to deal with massive amounts of information - it constantly creates a private map of the world to interact with. In other words, we could get lost in examining the black and orange fur... the lanky muscular body... the long canine teeth... and the deafening roar and intellectually brand the animal in front of us as *tiger*. Instead, we make a decision with the speed of *instinct*, and commence running for our lives.

The skills of discrimination, categorization, and abstraction, in this instance, are each invaluable to survival. It is quite natural for us to label the scary, large, orange and black, furry creature as a dangerous tiger. But is that really all it is? That creature was not born with a tag sewn under its tail that says *Scary Tiger – do not remove under penalty of law*. We gave it this recognized label: *tiger*. We also assign categories to the creature such as "mammal" and "feline" to help us all map *the idea* of *tiger*. Moreover, our shared experiences agree the tiger's attributes make it dangerous. Is it still necessary to be afraid of the creature if he is behind a cage at a zoo? Would he still be labeled a tiger if he were born mutated without striped fur or long, sabre-tooth fangs?

This animal is actually none of these things. Rather, interactions with such entities in the past give us a statistical model that society and culture have bought into - a cultural consensus for convenience and convention. We all live our lives believing the model or map of reality we construct *is reality itself.* Eastern philosophy and Western quantum physicists agree - we interact with an entire world that does not exist *except in our minds.*

This same dynamic holds true for the way we interact with people. Our minds have the same tendency to take past experiences and beliefs about individuals and create a template for certain types of people that permits us to react and to judge without additional information.

Take for instance, my own evolution. I lived with a mother who was very controlling and abusive. Therefore, every woman I sought to know intimately eventually came to represent my past-oriented mother model, regardless of the reality of the woman sitting across from me in the present.

Our strongest models of what to expect from others is developed from personal experiences during our most formative years as a child - before the age of seven. And, because we instinctively hold parents in such reverence, our models are overwhelmingly influenced by their behavior toward us. Our imaginary models include certain coping strategies that may have been helpful to us as defenseless children. However, holding on to those strategies long after we need them as adults can be very counter-productive. Such patterned behavior always restricts our ability to live in the moment.

What is more disconcerting is that our past-centered attitude toward people actually influences how people respond to us. In fact, our brains are *wired to connect,* according to Daniel Goleman in his book, *Social Intelligence: The New Science of Human Relationships.* We have neurons (aptly named *mirror neurons*) built specifically for empathy. As a consequence, our attitude toward someone will be registered by them regardless of whether we believe we are outwardly projecting that attitude or not. People tend to live up to our expectations of them, whether those expectations are informed or uninformed, conscious or unconscious.

All of this is to say that our experiences with people are greatly influenced by our attitude towards them, and our attitude towards them is most often influenced by our experiences as children.

The Buddhist take this a step farther with the belief that what is inside of us reflects what is outside of us, and visa versa. If you internally believe that people cannot be trusted, people you encounter in your outer world will betray you in a proportional manner. Conversely, If you believe that people at their core are pure love, you will see pure love exude, even from the cranky ones.

The Buddhist philosophy of inside = outside is now being confirmed in the arena of science at the most minute level of matter – the quantum level. This was clearly illustrated in Young's double slit experiment, as shown in Chapter Three. The experiment proved that light (the foundation of all matter) is a wave function that exists everywhere simultaneously until observed. Once observed, the wave collapses into particles with a position. Therefore, according to quantum physics, just the act of intelligently observing something affects it. Science has established that, indeed, our consciousness has the power to influence our environment!

If this food for thought is hard to palate, try an experiment. Think of someone in your life with whom you are currently experiencing friction. Before you see them again spend at least 15 minutes meditating on them being kind and positively responsive toward you. For this experiment to be successful you must actually allow yourself to *feel* what it would be like for them to respond to you in such a positive manner. Then the next time you meet that person look them in the eye and visualize them responding as you had them respond in your meditation. You may not hear the exact words you anticipated, but your results will always be proportional to how authentically you *felt* the desired response during your earlier meditation. This strategy can work to alter your experience of anyone in your life. And theirs, of yours.

You are your brother

The underlying theme behind all the quantum physics mentioned in this book is that essentially everything is connected. Everything is made of the same energy. Deepak Chopra describes our bodies as *energy with information*, much like the electrical current entering a computer that is converted into the information of 1's and 0's. The 1's and 0's are organized into more complex structures called programs. The programs allow us to interact with a reality that exists only inside our computers. Yet this reality is basically nothing but *energy with information*. Believe it or not, our physical reality works in a similar fashion.

If everything is connected and we are all made of the same energy, then it is safe to conclude that you are inextricably linked to your brother. (*Sisters! Brother is not a gender-specific term in this text.*) When you are connected to your brothers then everything you do to them you ultimately do to yourself. Let's extend the logic of that statement – *everything you see in your brother, you see in yourself*. Therefore, whenever you choose to see divinity in another, you will recognize divinity in yourself.

With this connection established, you can begin to comprehend the Buddhist principle of *non-judgment*. How can you judge anything or anyone that is a part of you? Judgment can only happen if there is a separation. If you believe you have been slighted by your brother, then you believe that you and your brother are separate. Moreover, the harsher the perceived slighting, the more distance you place between yourself, your brother, and your spiritual awakening.

According to Jesus, the only way to bridge that gap between yourself and the brother whom you perceived slighted you is to forgive him. I do not mean forgiveness as simply something you pronounce - not a heartless social utterance. True forgiveness requires a change in perspective. The change is from the conviction you have been slighted to believing that you are connected to the one who *supposedly* slighted you. Now, take that statement a step further - admit it - *YOU* were the one who created the slight originally when you projected whatever model that was in your own mind. This perspective represents the ultimate state of *internal locus of control,* meaning that *you* are responsible for everything that happens to *you*. In this state of forgiveness we validate that sense of responsibility and affirm our connection to the rest of mankind.

Ultimately, we are asked to recognize the same divinity in our brother that exists within ourselves. That divinity is our connection and the only reality that persists beyond those separating constructs of time and space.

The most important person to forgive is yourself

The forgiveness of others always starts with forgiving yourself, only because every quality of others that you hold judgment against is always a quality that you have not forgiven yourself for. For instance, if you hold a grudge against your roommate for not cleaning up the common areas to your standards, you can bet that cleanliness is something you judge yourself for quite harshly. Such judgment is even more pronounced if you consider yourself neat. Your psychic, value-laden charge around cleanliness is the pre-judicial force that compels you to be neat.

We can forgive ourselves for not making enough money, not being completely honest, or for not finishing writing that book. There are countless ways we hold judgment against ourselves and thereby block the vital energies critical for a coherent heart, successful manifestation, and more importantly, collective manifestation. Every instance of judgment against ourselves will ALWAYS be projected and perceived as judgment against others. We are all humans drowning in a sea of frailty. That simply means none of us are qualified to pass judgment, even on ourselves.

The fact that our actions carry value that is either positive or negative is rooted in the tenets of karma. However, karma is only karma when you believe in the negativity or positivity of your actions. Karma is overcome simply by knowing that all actions, supposedly good or bad, ultimately lead to God. Our awareness of this universal neutrality of action accelerates our journey to Source. Is it not ironic that your karmic journey always ends where it started?... with YOU!

Summary

Judgment and guilt are the most powerful blocks to energy flowing naturally through the chakras. This is especially true in your heart chakra. Forgiveness is one of the most powerful tools for clearing these blockages. In its truest form, Forgiveness is critical on the path toward realizing the profound connection to each other. Collective manifestation is impossible unless the walls of judgment that separate us are seen for the illusions that they are.

Inside = outside

- It is a biologically-evolved survival mechanism for humans to create a mental map or model of our world to cope with a ceaseless barrage of information in our present cultural environment.
- The moment you believe this mental map is actually the same territory it represents is the moment you leave this Present Reality to root around referencing The Past.

- To place your faith completely in the mental map also negatively affects our relationships with others, because you will tend to see them through the filtered lens of your past experiences rather than seeing them for who they are.
- Buddhists believe your context or environment always reflects what is going on inside of you. Our insides always reflect our outsides, and *visa versa*.

You are your brother

- Quantum physics reveals how matter is energy and everything and everyone is connected via this universally pervasive energy.
- If we accept the former premise as true, then all of us are at subatomic levels of reality *connected* rather than *separate* entities.
- If we are connected? Then anything we do to each other we ultimately do to ourselves.
- Disconnects exist in each and every mind. The most profoundly destructive disconnect is between you and those you perceive have sinned against you. Both Logic and Jesus instruct us that forgiveness is the only path to bridge that gap.
- Forgiveness is not a "sharing" of how you are no longer upset by sins against you. Forgiveness is a change of perspective, an understanding that your experience is your creation, even if that experience is one of *suffering* seemingly imposed by others.

The most important person to forgive is yourself

All our judgments against others are rooted in judgment of ourselves. Judgment of ourselves is the primary source of energetic blockage of the body's chakra system, therefore being an impediment to heart-centered manifestation.

Judging anything you do as *good* or *bad* chains us to the *cause* and *effect* cycle of karma. The Karmic cycle can only be resolved and overcome each time you act in service *to* others... *with* others.

Ultimately, forgiveness is your understanding of how it is impossible for a connected system to *sin against itself*. Whenever you see and agree everything truly *IS* part of one unified whole, the very concept of "sin" is realized as an utter illusion.

Exercises for Chapter 4

1. Go to your personal altar and begin to meditate. Pay close attention to your breath. On the inhale, hear the sound *hong*. When you exhale hear the sound *saw*. Focus on what happens to your heart space as you do this meditation for than more than 15 minutes. This *Hong Saw* breath will still your mind and open your heart. Please note - it is also possible to go out-of-body with this breath, so reserve *Hong Saw* only during meditation. [1]

2. When you have the *Hong Saw* technique down, use the breath during meditation to focus on someone in your life who (you believe) has deliberately harmed you... *Parent? Co-worker? Ex-Lover?* What may have caused this person to act this way with you? Imagine what their childhood must have been like. Recall how *you* once perceived *them* (especially an ex-lover) and how they may have responded to that "working model" of them in your head. As you repeat this visualization breathing exercise over time you will be able to move from a state of guilt and blame to a place of understanding. At that level, you can finally visualize yourself and the individual of your focus as *one being* with no separation between the two of you.

3. Sit in meditation and perform the *Hong Saw* breath for at least 15 minutes. Afterwards focus on your chakras, starting with your root chakra and ending with your 6th chakra or Ajna. Imagine each chakra as a golden ball of light as you move up to the Ajna, repeat the internal mantra *I am pure, I am Innocent*. Pay attention to chakras that present resistance during this mantra. These are places in your body that harbor guilt. Breath through these places imagining your breath cleansing the chakra of guilty emotions. See figure 4-1 for the positions of the chakras.

Figure 4-1 Location of the chakras

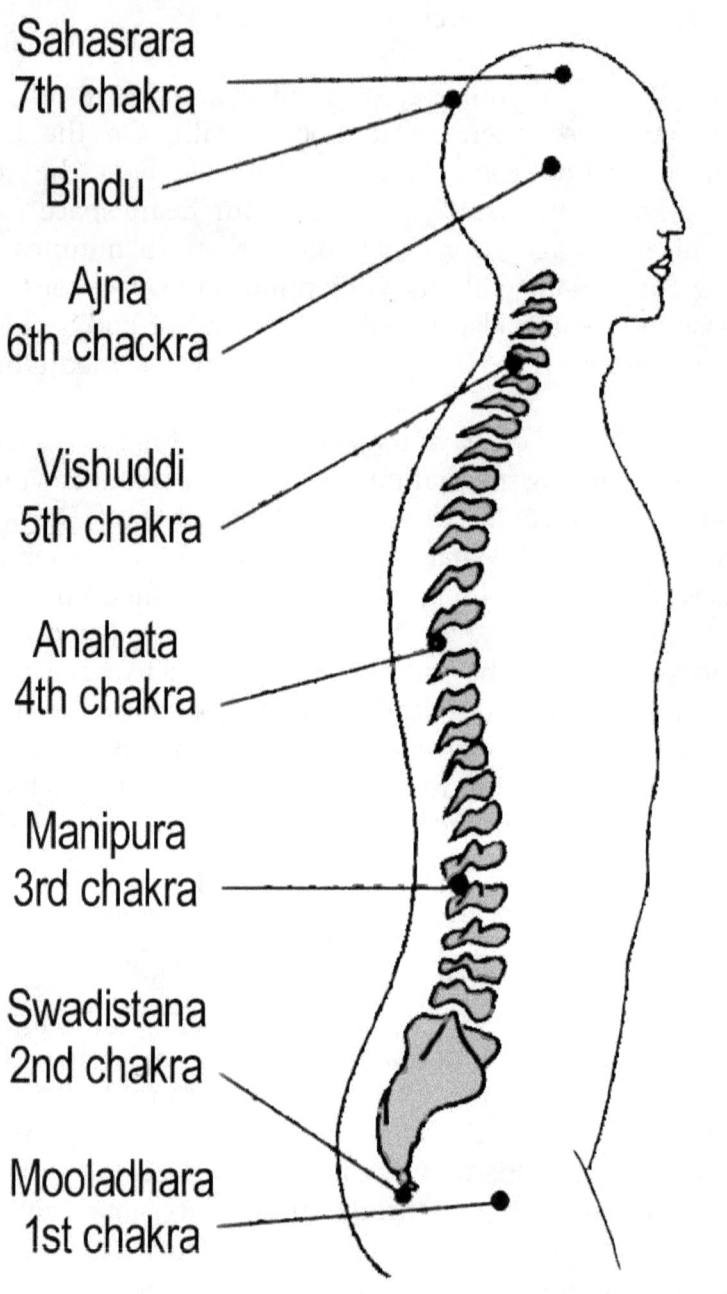

4. There are additional Paths which lead to the same enlightened state. If you are not already a devotee of *A Course in Miracles*[2] I highly suggest you make their workbook lessons a part of your daily routine. The Course is systematic way to change your perspective around forgiveness. I personally believe the Course is one of the most profound spiritual books ever written. Let's put it this way... if all the literature of the world were to be burned and I, alone, were tasked with choosing one book to keep for all of humanity... It would be *The Course in Miracles*.... Yes, I would even allow THIS very text to be lost in the sands of time in favor of *The Course*. However, if I could choose two books...

References

1. Saraswati, S. and Avinasha, B. (2002). *Jewel In The Lotus: The Tantric Path to Higher Consciousness.* Valley Village, CA. Ipsalu Publishing.

2. Schucman, H. (1976). *A course in miracles.* Mill Valley, CA. Foundation for Inner Peace.

5

Manifesting in the Eternal Moment

Years ago when I studied Zen Buddhism in Japan, my roshi would set aside time during meditation for us to sit and discuss our current difficulties with the practice. Nine times out of ten, I would go on and on about how my whole life was so damaged by the abuse I suffered as a child. I worried about whether I would be able to maintain a healthy, long-term relationship in the future.

One day, after patiently enduring another session of my endless angst, my roshi gently grabbed my arm and led me outside. He took a long, straight branch from the garden and stuck it into the ground. He held on to the stick and said "This stick is the present." He then pointed to the shadow of the stick created by the afternoon sun and said, "That is the past. The morning sun will project a shadow in the other direction. We can call that shadow the future." He looked me in the eyes with his matter-of-fact expression of love and patience and said. "The only thing that is real, whether it be morning or afternoon, is this stick. Yet, you insist on living in the shadows."

The Science and Practice of Manifesting Unity Consciousness

My Grasshopper Moment... I will never forget that lesson. In fact, it is one lesson that keeps on giving because, as I continue to evolve, I recognize more and more the gravity of his words. We miss too much of our lives focused on everything except each precious moment we are given.

The next time you drive down the street, notice how many people in a group are isolated with their cell phones. The next time you go shopping, notice how many times you are acknowledged with eye contact. The next time you make love, notice where your mind wanders or retreats. The next time a child asks you to play, notice if you have any hesitation or doubt. The next time you return home from work, notice what you tend to do first and how long it takes you to feel at home. Did you notice? Staying present is not a characteristic of our modern culture.

Our society has evolved to an unprecedented place technologically. In this faster-paced, digital reality we have the power to communicate across the globe, yet personal conversations today are less relevant, constantly interrupted by the next text message or ringtone. Hundreds of cable channels show us the world, yet most of us do not really know our neighbor. We have succumbed to our fantastic toys - those perfect instruments of distraction and avoidance to make us immortal, invisible, and isolated.

When you distract yourself, it means you are not comfortable with what is happening in the moment. When you are not happy with the moment, it usually means you are not happy with your circumstance. When you are not happy with your circumstance, you are obviously unhappy with yourself. If only there were some diversion....

Being present is the only way to cope with any context that seems disagreeable. Being present is the only way to gain access to whatever really needs to be dealt with inside. Being present dissolves the linear construct separating cause and effect, so that your past, present, and future can merge into one timeless moment. It is in this eternal moment that we are freed from the constraints of time and can manifest beyond being bound to one event having to create another. Before we can awaken to the manifesting power within this eternal moment, we must first recognize the true nature of time.

What Is Time?

To be succinct - Time is a construct... something manmade. We constructed it because time helps us deal more conveniently with a world we have also engineered for our convenience. "Time is money"? Whoever said that has no respect for the value of time.

However, not every culture places the same degree of importance on time. The spectrum of time consciousness finds one extreme in American culture, which regards time as the fuel that drives the Puritan work ethic that built our society. We are always on the clock. Productivity measures how much profit we can make per minute. Whereas, on the other side of the time consciousness spectrum, an Amazonian tribe, for instance, may only recognize time in terms of cycles of nature. Things happen much slower and with more impulse in such societies. Ancient Buddhist and Hindu traditions define the construct of time so well, pioneer psychologists and modern physicists both use the same esoteric vocabulary to explore exactly how our ego uses time to maintain its persuasive perception of separation.

Buddhist perspective of time

To most of us, time is linear and rigid, so obvious how it orchestrates everything from the movement of the Cosmos to events of our lives. However, the Buddhists insist time in the linear sense is an illusion, created by man to deal with the universe as mapped out by our ego. To Buddhists, time is more fundamental - like a wheel or a cycle.

The Science and Practice of Manifesting Unity Consciousness

Dirk Vorenkamp, Assistant Professor of Religious Studies at Lawrence College, teaches the Buddhist concept of time as a wheel. His most lucid example is from Buddhist philosopher Fa-tsang (643-712 CE), who taught how time is both an infinite number of events as well as the whole collection of those events. Like a wheel, all events in time are simultaneously a unity of past, present, and future. Fa-tsang believed that every event of time was influenced by both those events that came before as well as those events that came afterward, but all of this happens simultaneously rather than on the linear track we follow. Time just flows; from past to present, from future to present, and past to future, all simultaneously.

Like something from an old Star Trek episode, scientific experiments validate Fa-tsang's notion of time. In 1976, German-born Helmut Schmidt conducted an experiment in which people focused on previously-generated random numbers, then asked to concentrate on an increased frequency of the number 4 out of a previously generated random string ranging from one to four. When the tapes were later reviewed they showed a larger than statistically predicted number of 4's. The accepted analysis determined the subjects had retroactively influenced the random generation of those numbers on the punch tape. Time moved from future to past. [1] Schmidt conducted experiments in 1993 with theoretical physicist Henry Stapp. In these experiment subjects were able to retroactively influence the rate of decay of radioactive isotopes. [2]

The Buddhist concept of time also includes the idea of impermanence. Have you heard the adage: There is never a moment when you can stick your foot in the same river twice? Time is, indeed, more like a river. However, our mind shapes the riverbed, each moment strung together in a linear trough of cause and effect. The question is: Could you ever separate one of those moments from the string? This is, of course, impossible.

We, ourselves, are also like the living river... more than

60% water! Every moment, our physical selves grow and decay replacing nearly every cell in our bodies over the next two years... with the exception of brain cells. Our brains age with us, atrophy without stimulation and exercise, and map our own synapses to be familiar, convenient, and "set in their ways".

The next question: Are we ever the same person at any given moment? The answer is: yes and no. There are no distinguishable moments except for the one we are currently in... the Eternal Moment. When we free ourselves from the mental prison of time we begin to realize that we are not a collection of moments from our past. Instead of working so hard to create a happy ending to our life's story, why not write your own script or transcend time and the story all together!

Hindu Perspective of Time

According to the Hindu theory of creation, time (Sanskrit 'kal') is a manifestation of God (Kali). Whenever God becomes active, Creation begins. Creation ends when God's energy returns to a state of inactivity. To the Hindus, God is timeless because the relative nature of time ceases to exist in the Absolute. "The past, the present and the future coexist in Him simultaneously."[3] Does this concept resonate with the Buddhist conception of time?

God creates the cycles of time, called Kalchakra. They create the illusion of division and linear movement through life and sustain the illusion of birth and death. However, whenever we are enlightened, we can see past these divisions and experience the timeless nature of God.

Putting It All Together

Regardless of the traditions previously discussed, one basic thing is true - all suffering is rooted in time. Suffering is, in its essence, a sustained resistance to the present. We find ourselves locked into models from the past with its attendant pain, guilt, or regret. Or, looking "ahead", we become anxious about the future, its dangers, anticipating every imaginable Fortune both Good and Bad. Past or Future? Either choice shuts out the present reality.

As creative beings, to manifest we must imagine what is being created actually exists in the present moment. If you attempt to manifest something by asking for it to happen sometime in the future, you are affirming your belief in the barrier of cause and effect. This denies your abilities to manifest any event without some other event that was "supposed to" come before it. Welcome back to where you started... still a billiard ball on the pool table of life, awaiting the bruising shocks of external action and reaction.

Summary

Contemporary society is far too attached to the construct of time. We are always too busy either reliving our past in the misery of victim-hood or desiring something imaginary in our future. Scientifically and spiritually, both past and future are illusions. Only the present moment is real. It is when we immerse ourselves in this moment that we are truly free to manifest without the constraints of time-bound cause and effect.

Buddhist perspective

- Time is like a wheel. It has no beginning or end, no birth or death.
- Time has an impermanent nature. Everything is constantly changing. Therefore there are no such things as *moments* in the past or future simply because these moments cannot be separated from the eternal moment of the present.

- Time can flow backwards as well as forwards. Science has given us ample quantum evidence of this phenomenal reality.

Hindu perspective

- God manifests time to give us the illusion of division, birth and death... all for the purpose of spiritual growth.
- The fundamental nature of time is clearly expressed in cycles.
- When one becomes enlightened, they see through the illusion of time, and transcend birth and death.

Exercises for Chapter 5

1. This exercise works best when you are at your busiest. Set your watch or your cell phone alarm to any peak time in the middle of your day. When the alarm sounds, stop everything you are doing and find a seat. Do at least 5 Hong Saw breaths, then look around you. Notice the smallest details of the environment, witness every sublime color, and hearken to each subtle sound, and meditate upon the beauty you ignore in span of each day.

And never forget - it is within your natural power to live every moment of your life completely immersed in the present.

References

1. Schmidt, Helmut J. (1976). PK Effect on Pre-Recorded Targets. *The Journal for the American Society for Psychical Research*. Volume 70, July 1976. pp. 267-291.

2. Schmidt, Helmut J. and Stapp, Henry P. (1993). Study of PK with Pre-Recorded Random Events and the Effect of Pre-Observation. *Journal of Parapsychology*. Volume 57. 1193. pp. 331-348.

3. http://hinduism.about.com/library/weekly/aa012101a.htm

4. http://hinduism.about.com/library/weekly/aa012101a.htm

The Power of the Collective

Modern Man has mapped out a cultural model that depends upon us to each think of our Self as separated, isolated, and, ideally, independent. This time-driven, self-absorbed mind-set has become so pervasive that most of us remain oblivious to everything of true value around us. Right down to the suffering of our next door neighbor, let alone any starving soul in some yonder land. Behold such irony! Never before has civilization been more inter-connected and inter-dependent than today. When we rise above our isolated bubbles of homes, cars, and cubicles, we see and comprehend higher levels of larger *natural* organization we may utilize together to create a more blissful life.

Imagine yourself floating above your home in a hot air balloon. Looking down, you would see systems of interconnected roads, freeways, and power lines that resemble an integrated electronic circuit board. But this would only describe the technology that connects us physically. What your eyes can't see is the global wireless system that allows my friend from Africa to communicate via cellphone with his brother hoeing a field in a rural village 200 miles outside Kampala. Now, with the internet, we can exchange information with such speed and depth that it boggles even the modern mind. Yet... many of us still believe we are independent, isolated, and alone.

Every time an extraterrestrial biologist observes life on Earth, they must conclude the true nature of our dominant species is that of a hive mentality, able to function as a unit with impressive agility and speed. One human isolated from the collective would be useless, eventually weaken, and ultimately die, as if you isolated an ant from its colony or honey bee from its hive.

The truth is that we are desperately dependent on one another, not as tribes, or castes, or faiths, or nations, but on a planetary level. Our salvation as a species has never and will never come from the accomplishments of individuals as the study of history would make us believe. Our future is truly dependent upon the least of us.

Our current, pervasive information technology is really nothing more than metaphors for the far more powerful spiritual connections we all share. Our positive, authentic energetic connection can spread more quickly across the human hive by communicating through the frequency of love.

This spiritually energetic connection begins first on the individual level when we choose to live in a state of unconditional love, where our own heart attains a state of coherence as mentioned in Chapter Two. The second step occurs when awakened hearts of individuals are then aligned in a state of conscious, *collective* coherence. Only then, when heart-based intention is added to the agreement, anything imaginable becomes possible. This is the purpose behind Collective Heart Yoga (CHY). The work of Dr. David Hawkins offers us a glimpse into the power of focused awareness operating at the level of love.

Dr. David Hawkins and the levels of consciousness

David Hawkins conducted thousands of kinesthetic (muscle testing) trials to measure levels of conscious evolution. He had a scale from 1 to 1000. In 2002, he contended that only 15% of the world's population was over the level of 200. Note that scores below 200 in his States of Consciousness Chart range from guilt, apathy, grief, and fear, to desire, anger, pride... then peak at courage. The more enlightened end of the spectrum looks like this:

Table 6-1 Levels of Consciousness over 200

Enlightenment	700 - 1000
Peace	600
Love	500
Reason	400
Acceptance	350
Willingness	310
Neutrality	250
Courage	200

Its important to note that every increase of a level is not linear; it yields an exponential gain on a logarithmic scale. In other words, 200 is not twice that of 100; it is 10 to the 200th power (10^{200}). And *THAT* is clearly an abundance of energy to draw upon.

Dr. Hawkins estimated the conscious level of the entire population to be at 207 in 2002. This is not to be confused with I.Q. Our *Collective Enlightment Quotient* in the growth of human consciousness has been exponential since then. That level of 207 represents an actual *tipping point*, having attained sufficient courage and clarity to no longer be subject to all the lower levels below 200... those eerie emotional levels that feel all too real while riding the Buddhist wheel of suffering that

The Science and Practice of Manifesting Unity Consciousness

binds a consciousness to the cycle of karma (Hell, Hunger, Animality, Anger, and Happiness).

Collectively, we have broken that cycle, as a species if not yet a culture. This Gift is being given for a very rare opportunity; one that comes around once every 26 thousand years, or so. Pick a date? I suggest *now!*

Your *individual* opportunity is to exercise our *collective* power, and amplify our intention to finally transcend our primal, insecure, violent ways, so we can all share the experience of an entirely new and vastly more expanded consciousness.

As mentioned earlier, levels of consciousness are exponential, much like the Richter scale for earthquake measurement. So, according to Dr. Hawkins' measurements, a consciousness at the level of 500 can counteract the energy of 750,000 individuals at levels below 200. The level of 500 is significant because most souls attracted to the practice of collective manifestation are at or entering this level. Dr. Hawkins describes the 500 level :

> *Just as the level 200 demarcates a critical change of consciousness, 500 is a point at which awareness makes another giant leap. Although survival of the individual is still important, the motivation of Love begins to color all activities, and creativity comes into full expression, accompanied by commitment, dedication, and expressions of charisma. Here, excellence is common in every field of human endeavor, from sport to scientific investigation. Altruism becomes a motivating factor, along with dedication to principles. Leadership is accepted rather than sought. From this level, great music, art, and architecture emerge. as does the capacity to uplift others by one's mere presence.*
>
> *In the upper 500's inspirational leaders who set an example for the rest of society are found and, in their respective fields, create new paradigms with their far-reaching implications for mankind. Although well aware*

themselves that they still have defects and limitations, people on this level are often seen by the general public as out of the ordinary...Many people in the mid 500s begin to have spiritual experiences of profound import and become immersed in spiritual pursuit. Some astonish their friends and families with sudden breakthroughs into new, subjective contexts of reality. Consciousness at this level can be described as vision and may focus on uplifting society as a whole. (Hawkins, 1995, pg 99-100)

Once your score tops 600, you are in a stage of complete, unconditional love. According to Dr. Hawking's scale, one loving thought contains the power of $10^{-10 \text{million}}$ microwatts, whereas any fearful thought generates only $10^{-750 \text{million}}$ microwatts. Those of you who remember how negative exponents work will clearly see that our power of love is significantly more charged that of fear. As adherents of love's path, the time has come to project our power as a focused, coherent collective, thereby exponentially influencing the evolution of consciousness on this planet.

Achieving a state of collective coherence

Entrainment is what happens when all the pendulums in a clock store eventually swing in unison. The vibration of one human mind can be entrained with other minds, achieving a collective state of peak focus.

There are many examples of how native cultures achieve a collective state of peak focus to carry out remote healing. Consistently, the beat of a drum proves to be the most effective in causing the brain to slow down into a trance state. A drum is used to both entrain the brain and synchronize certain breathing activities in Collective Heart Yoga.

Mantra

If you prefer to *see* evidence of the creative, organizing power of sound, try this: 1) place a metal plate atop a reclined loudspeaker; 2) cover the plate with fine sand; 3) generate a loud single frequency or pure note of sound under a the metal plate. This results in the creation of very interesting sand designs on what's called a *Chladni Disk*. With increasing pitch, sustained harmonics, and resonance, very intricate designs begin to appear on the plate. Each time the frequency of the sound is changed, the sand goes through a fluid transition and ultimately arranges itself into another beautiful, static pattern. The higher the audio frequency, the more complex the design. Below is the design that is produced when sounding the vowel A in sand. Yogis have long used such designs as geometric representations of sacred sounds called *yantras* and focus on them during meditation to awake certain chakras.

Figure 6-1   The vowel A in sand

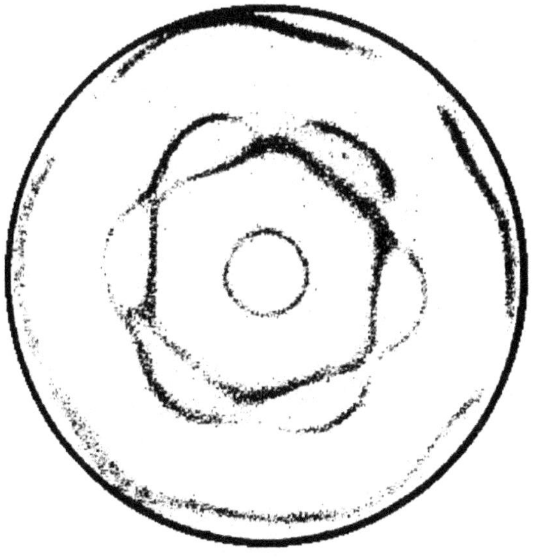

Just as sound projected through a Chladni disk organizes a pile of sand into a beautiful yantra, man's current consciousness is the relatively simple pattern in sand that, through mantra, will transform into a more complex, stable geometry. Just as an individual consciousness can be transformed through mantra, so can our collective consciousness be transformed through the practice of entrainment and collective, resonant mantra.

I mentioned the word resonant. To clarify, resonance is the tendency of a system to oscillate at larger amplitude or magnitude. Atmospheric vibration, or sound, reaches its highest magnitude with a specific pitch. Which pitch is the correct pitch? It differs, depending on the chamber in which you make the sound.

In Collective Heart Yoga, there is a period towards the end of the practice where all the participants are sounding single seed (bija) mantras while performing both the emanating heart cobra breath and manifestation cobra breath (see Chapter 9 - The Practice). What is critical is that participants surrender all "ownership" of their individual mantras by either raising or lowering their pitch to achieve an overall resonance within the group harmonic. This necessary surrendering happens only when the participants recognize when their overtone becomes resonant, and then remain aware whether their own individual voice is adding to or detracting from that collective harmonic.

Initial recognition of this resonance occurs when participants are positioned back-to-back. In my personal practice, paring male and female is most productive with the added balance of Shiva and Shakti. First, the duo performs a special *Cobra* breath together, individually raising or lowering their pitch until they achieve resonance in their own duet. After this pairing, the same thing is done within a trio or group of three. Ideally, one member of the opposite sex is represented in each trio for some degree of gender balance. Seat the trio with their backs positioned in a triangular fashion (as shown in a top view in figure 6-2):

Figure 6-2 Trio cobra breathing configuration

When the trio achieves resonance they are ready to be placed in sacred geometric patterns along with all the other trios. Figure 6-3 (next page) shows the largest recommended arrangement of participants. A six-pointed star is the traditional symbol for the heart. The down-pointing triangle represents Shiva (masculine energy). Up-pointing triangles represents Shakti (female energy).

If there are more than 18 participants, divide by 3 and group into star configurations. Please note that certain numbers of participants do not lend themselves to sacred geometries which integrate trios exclusively. While mathematics seem perfect, people are not. So never allow rigid ritual to take away from the effectiveness of the session. See Appendix A for additional arrangements based on number of participants.

Figure 6-3 Configuration of 18 participants along sacred geometry

The earlier definition of resonance was confined to sound produced by mantras during the last phase of the practice. Even your heartiest chant will not go far beyond the meditation room. Yet a deeper exploration of resonance reveals that, in coherent systems, one object may set another distant object into motion if it shares a sympathetic type of frequency. This is what happens when you strike a tuning fork of a certain frequency and bring it in the field of another tuning fork tuned of sympathetic frequency. The untouched tuning fork will begin to vibrate as if it had been struck.

The sound resonance that is achieved in the room during the Collective Heart Yoga is only an initiatory resonance that is meant to set off a resonance in a sympathetic frequency far beyond our senses' normal capacity to measure. This resonance happens in the frequency of thought or intention which is of a frequency much higher than that of even light and travels far beyond the practice room. Through the practice of collective manifestation, the frequency of intention is amplified by a room in coherence filled with individual hearts in coherence. This projection of amplified, collective healing intention, then resonates with a similar frequency on the etheric level within the collective unconscious, therefore affecting us all.

Bija mantras

Below are the seed sounds of the chakras or bija mantras and the vowel sounds that are utilized in Collective Heart Yoga. The M in the seed sounds represents the maternal aspect of the universe which is material. The A sound represents the nonmaterial or the Paternal.

Table 6-2

Chakra	Sanskrit	Seed sound	Vowel	Vowel Sound	color
Seven	Sahasrara	no mantra	no sound	no sound	violet
Six	Ajna	OM	AYE / E	"ahh-eee"	Indigo
Five	Vishuddi	HAM	EYE / I	"I"	bright - blue
Four	Anahata	YAM	AH / A	"father"	green
Three	Manipura	RAM	OH	"go"	yellow
Two	Swadhisthana	VAM	OOO / O	"you"/"ewe"	orange - red
One	Muladhara	LAM	UH / U	"huh"	deep red

Targeting our collective unconscious

The most powerful way to directly influence the overall level of humanity's consciousness is through communication employing our *collective unconscious*. In the terms of its

pioneer practitioner, transcendent psychologist Carl Jung:
> *The collective unconsciousness commands the very nature of our existence by the act of consensus. We agree to a common understanding about a lot of reality. It is only within the small slices of human experience that we live outside that collective... some call those moments... miracles.*

Jung saw that man possesses layered levels of consciousness. (*figure 6-4, next page*)

- *Ego* - primarily concerned with taking care of the body. The ego selects, sorts, filters, and interprets our day to day trickle of sensory input called experience.
- *Unconscious* - extends beyond our ego's awareness. Seldom glimpsed, often repressed, in a much deeper, darker lake swimming with repressed memories and shadow aspects of the psyche.
- *Collective unconscious* - is never conscious and has no basis in experience. This part of the unconscious is not individual. It is global - perhaps universal. This deepest layer of psyche exists more like a vast ocean spanning the *symbolic* experience uniting all mankind. This collective experience is represented across cultures as *archetypes*. Archetypes embody the iconic role models of Humanity's experience, like Mother Earth, Father Sky, Hero, Trickster, and multiple Trinities.

Meditating upon these archetypes is a powerful way to access our collective unconscious. Native cultures skillfully use them to orchestrate the deepest and most powerful form of intention and initiation on their collective, tribal level. Father Sky and Mother Earth, Cosmic Shiva and Cosmic Shakti are among the oldest archetypes, used often in CHY during the *emanating heart* and *manifestation cobras* as well as during the *unity breath* to open the heart.

Figure 6-4 Jung's Layers of Consciousness

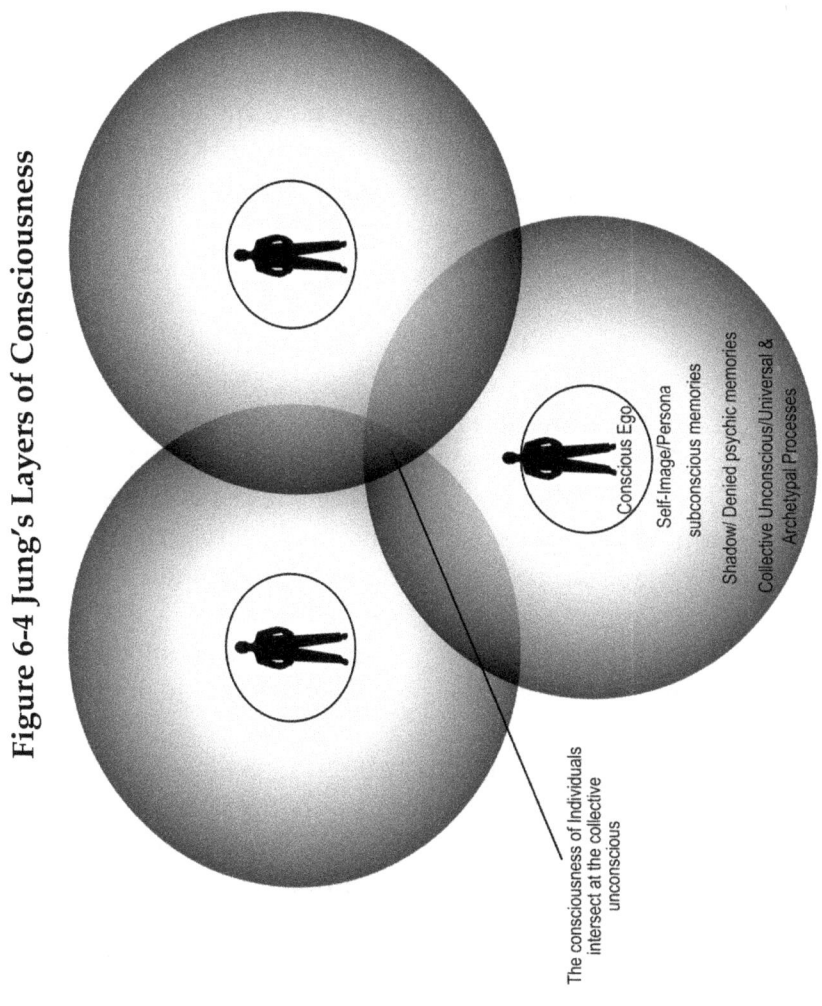

Our changing Planet: Apocalypse or collective opportunity

I suppose it's no longer a secret to anyone that the planet is experiencing a great shift. Similar cycles have happened before and bring about profound changes in the collective unconsciousness of mankind. One physical sign of this shift is peak solar activity and corresponding changes in the magnetic field of the Earth. We are currently at the beginning of Solar Cycle 24, which could prove to be one of the most unusual cycles to date.

The Global Coherence Initiative

There are now researchers who believe that humans, acting collectively, can affect geomagnetic activity. The Global Coherence Initiative, an offshoot of the prestigious HeartMath Institute, is networking highly precise magnetic sensors around the planet to prove the following hypotheses.

- Hypothesis No. 1: All living things are interconnected and we communicate with each other via biological and electromagnetic fields.
- Hypothesis No. 2: Not only are humans affected by planetary energetic fields, but conversely the earth's energetic systems are also influenced by collective human emotions and consciousness. Much of the planetary field environment is made up of the collective consciousness of the inhabitants.
- Hypothesis No. 3: Large numbers of people intentionally creating heart-coherent states of care, love, compassion and appreciation can generate a coherent standing wave that will help offset the current planetary wave of stress, discord and incoherence.

The second Hypothesis is supported by the work of Roger Nelson at Princeton. His team accesses a world-wide network of random number generators. They have monitored the levels of randomness over time and identified instances and conditions in which human consciousness has indeed affected the global field. In fact, the highest documented fluctuation of randomness occurred during the attacks on the World Trade Center, September 11, 2001. It is significant to note that there was a significant fluctuation in randomness three hours prior to the attack. Does this suggests that humanity, on the whole, had a collective intuition of the impending tragedy?

Figure 6-6 is data from satellites measuring Earth's magnetic field during the hours surrounding the 9/11 attacks. At the same time, there was also an increase in the Earth's magnetic field, yet another possible indication of the impact of our collective consciousness on the magnetic field of the Earth.

Figure 6-5 [1]

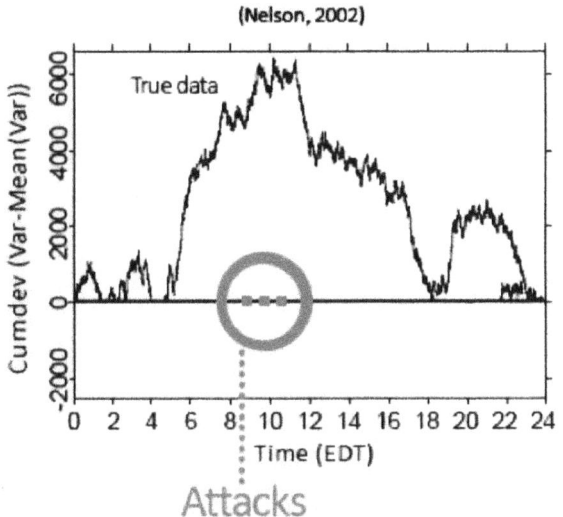

Evidence of Collective Intuition: RNG Data from GCP Sites Around the World per 9/11/01 Terrorist Attacks
(Nelson, 2002)

Figure 6-6[1]

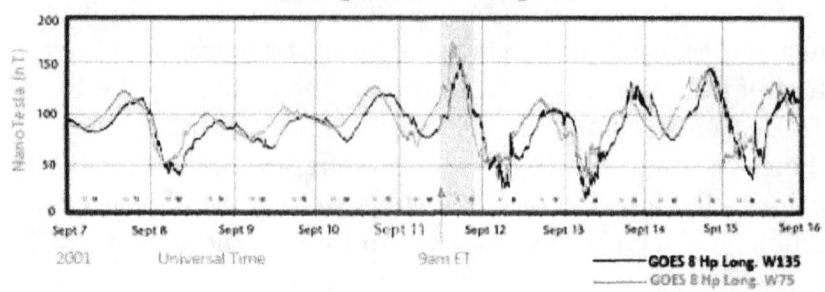

A similar fluctuation in the random number generator and the Earth's magnetic field happened during the President Obama's inauguration ceremony, indicating the potential influence of a more positive collective consciousness, as shown in figures 6-7 and 6-8.

Figure 6-7 [2]

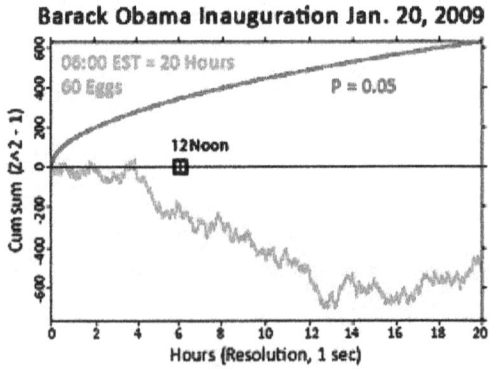

Edgar Cayce's advice on the solar cylces

Edgar Cayce, the famous psychic, believed the collective meditation of humanity could even affect the solar cycles and, moreover, the welfare of mankind. In Cayce's own words:

> *Sunspots, as well as earth changes, are reflections of our own state of consciousness, a result of our own actions, the boomerang of divine law. Sunspots are reflections of the 'turmoil and strife' that we ourselves have created, and our own mind is 'the builder.' The responsibility for Earth changes lies squarely on our shoulders, and how we conduct our relationships with others has everything to do with the changing face of the earth. Earth changes are 'adjustments' that have to be made because something is out of alignment. Just as we create chaotic conditions by our own out-of-alignment behavior, so we can create positive transformation by our loving attitudes and actions. (Reading #5757-1)*

Exercises for Chapter 6

1. Nadi Shadhona is a yogic practice that synchronizes left and right hemispheres.

- Place tip of index finger between your eyebrows.
- Use the thumb and the 2nd (middle) finger to alternately close the right and left nostril.
- Close right nostril with thumb and *inhale* through the left nostril.
- Release thumb from right nostril and use the 2nd finger to close left nostril.
- *Exhale* through the right nostril.
- Holding fingers in same position, *inhale* through the right nostril.
- Close right nostril with thumb, remove 2nd finger and *exhale* through left nostril.
- Repeat alternations for at least 5 minutes.

2. Ko Hum meditation. The Ko Hum meditation is a tantric exercise that also synchronizes left and right hemispheres of the brain. Some camps say that "Ko Hum" mean "What am I?" Others translate the mantra as meaning "I am that." Regardless of the translation, by following the steps below, you will experience an incredible union within yourself that will allow more opening to union with the Collective.

- Visualize a golden sphere of light residing in your left brain's hemisphere
- Inhale and intone the internal mantra, KO.
- Visualize the golden sphere of light traveling to your right hemisphere.
- Once the sphere of light has reached your right hemisphere, internally intone the mantra, HUM

The Science and Practice of Manifesting Unity Consciousness

- Visualize the golden sphere of light traveling back to your left hemisphere and repeat the cycle by silently intoning the mantra, KO.
- Each time you complete a cycle count down 100, 99, 98, 97... until you reach 0. If you make a mistake in your count... start over. The counting keeps your mind from wandering in the stratosphere.

References

1. Annette Deyhle, Commentaries On the Global Coherence monitoring systems. http://www.glcoherence.org/monitoring-system/commentaries.html

2. About the Global Coherence monitoring system. http://www.glcoherence.org/monitoring-system/about-system.html

3. www.cymatronsoundhealing.com/_wsn/page4.html

Deyhle, A and McCraty, R. (2010) *The Global Coherence Initiative*. January edition of *Energy Magazine*.

Hawkins, D. R. (1995) *Power vs force: The hidden determinants of human behaviour*. Veritas Publishing, Sedona, Az.

Judith, A. (1987) *Wheels of life: A user's guide to the chakra system*. Llewellyn Publications, Woodbury, MN.

Enlisting Help From Your Personal Connection to The Divine

Most of us are still struggling with this three dimensional existence, so have little experience with conscious manifestation. The majority of our experiences essentially vomit out from our unconscious while we navigate our lives through the sick mess we've created. This remains the reality for entities who have yet to realize the true creative power of their thoughts and feelings. At some point in the evolution of any sentient life, there is a connection with the energy center (chakra) that represents the midpoint between planetary and heavenly energy - the most ancient being *Shiva and Shakti energy*. This pivotal midpoint is the heart chakra - *the Anahata*.

Most of our collective human experience has been a real fight to possess and stockpile survival resources. Yet, once the heart chakra is activated, we begin a new journey of creating and giving. Accessing the Anahata marks the end of our struggle to simply survive and exist for another day.

In fact, our courage and vitality becomes strengthened by the level of altruism or unselfishness in our giving. As our journey of giving progresses into altruism, we actually evolve beyond our familiar third dimension into authentic realms we once could barely fathom.

Throughout history we find individuals who have traveled far on this journey of giving. Some are still residing with us; many more are active in our lives from behind the dimensional veil. Westerners label them *angels, avatars, totems,* and *saints* - whose own spiritual growth is dependent upon how much they give unto us. Their primary task - their avowed purpose - is to guide us to become better givers and, as a consequence, more conscious manifestors... knowing, then demonstrating how giving and manifestation go hand-in-hand.

In the practice of Collective Heart Yoga (CHY), you will call upon your own personal connection to the Divine to bridge the gap between what you believe you're capable of manifesting and what your collective is asked to manifest. So it is critical that you first determine the identity of your divine emissary; *then* you can begin to develop an ongoing practice to strengthen your connection to that entity on a daily basis.

Identifying your divine emissary

"Belief" in itself is an individual, experiential, metaphysical concept. Whether you realize it yet or not, each of us has a personal connection to at least one of these evolved entities. It is often a figure from our cultural or religious upbringing. Here, I call them *personal connections to the divine* or our *divine emissaries*. This is the *kindred* spirit that resonates instantly in your heart. Some of you may already know who your divine emissary is. Many do not. When you are ready, I *guarantee* it is not difficult to initiate your own resonant connection.

The first thing to do is simply ask: *Who is my divine*

emissary?, together with this invitation: *Please make yourself known to me.* To be sure, your request must be genuinely from the heart. (As you know - half-hearted efforts only yield half-baked results.)

It is understandable to have fear regarding this connection. Yet it is important to know that these entities can only intervene in your life if you ask them to. They are very careful to express themselves only in ways that will not engender fear. These are not dead ghosts; they are Living Spirits. Their sole purpose is to facilitate your evolution as a creator. Imposing their will or their presence upon you is contrary to that purpose.

As a child, I would talk to Jesus as if he were my imaginary friend. When I grew older, I rejected the strictest Baptist tenets that swore the good shepherd would throw you to the wolves if you chose to explore any other path beyond the narrow Fundamental way. I could never understand how my dear friend, Jesus, could permit my adoptive parents to be so cruel. When I finally left home and joined the Navy, I rejected Jesus as a complete myth, along with all the other stories of the Bible.

It wasn't until I was in my forties that I again felt a compelling need to look outside myself for help. I was still "spiritual" in the manner of a healer, trying to insert my own brand of emotional healing deep into the psyche of someone I cared about personally as well as professionally. Her issue was so buried that our efforts to identify a pivotal event of her childhood had exhausted us both. I was then advised by a mentor to ask for assistance from my "personal connection to the divine". I had no idea what he was talking about.

Because my heart was at last back in my work, I probed my (over) educated mind to see which "evolved entity" felt at all connected to me. My logical mind suggested Babaji Nagaraj, the inspiration of many wise tantra instructors. Not to mention, Babaji was honorably showcased on my personal alter. So I asked Babaji for help... *and got nothing*. Despondent and again disillusioned, my mentor guided me to look within my heart rather than my mind.

So I followed my mentor's advice. I went deep into my heart and came face to face with....Jesus! Yes, awaiting me was the same entity I had rebuked for the vast majority of my life. Except it was not *their* Jesus. This was *my* Jesus. I gratefully asked for light to enter the psyche of the woman I was trying to help. Almost instantly she began to cry with all of her body, while my mind's eye saw a scared little girl near a fire. Following that session she intimated that she remembered being badly burned on an old heater when she was barely two years old. She had effectively blocked it from rising into her conscious mind from that moment until this one; the very moment I realized that Jesus was, indeed, my very own, "personal connection to the Divine."

Of course my new-and-improved Jesus was no longer the same judgmental deity I was ordered to obey in the Baptist Church. You, too, may find that a rejected entity from your own innocent childhood may prove to be your divine emissary, due, in great part, to the psychic charge you invested in them in your formative years.

To this day, I have had no preternatural visits from dear old Babaji. My partner at the time, Connie, also maintains his likeness on her personal alter. She even had a life-changing encounter with him during a jog in forest. And she always displayed a much smaller and tattered picture of the avatar than I kept on my alter. That just goes to show that our divine emissaries are more a matter of our hearts than our brains. *Though, just in case you're listening, Babaji, I'm still waiting to hear from you.*

How to nurture the connection with your divine emissary

Nurturing a trusting relationship with your divine emissary is all about falling in love with that entity. Understanding that all these entities are the more evolved aspects of your own consciousness, I am essentially insisting you must fall in love with yourself. Your love must be willingly, faithfully, and eagerly affirmed on a daily basis. Build a simple altar within your space. Place a representation of your avatar upon it. Choose and use with joy any prayer or chant you find historically connected to your divine entity.

For damaged doubters and healthy skeptics alike, I cannot emphasize this following point often enough: Eternal "God" is One Energy - *with six billion Names, six billion Voices, six billion Faces*. No matter which Divine Avatar inspires your heart to resonate, you are wisely, simply, and always choosing an aspect of your Higher Self.

Figure 7-1 (next page) is a list featuring some key Western and Eastern entities well-known for their positive archetypal influences, together with their backgrounds and relevant prayers or chants. Of course, what's listed here is only a fraction of the evolved entities that can be called upon at any time to assist in your own evolution as a creator.

The Master Is In.....You!

Table 7-1 Avatars

Name	Background	Methods of Invocation
Babaji (Nagaraj)	Born in India around 203AD, He became immortal through the practice of Siddha Yoga and medicine. He has taught the cobra breath to be passed down in a secret oral tradition. Babaji remains on this Earthly plane to help mankind evolve.	mantra - Om Kriya Babaji Namah Aum
Jesus	Jew born in Bethlehem around 5AD. He taught unconditional love through the path of forgiveness.	perform acts of selfless service.
Krishna	an incarnation of Vishnu. Born around July 21, 3228 BCE	Hare Krishna Mantra - "Hare Krishna, Hare Krishna, Krishna Krishna, Hare Hare Hare Rama, Hare Rama, Rama Rama, Hare Hare"
Mary Mother of Jesus	Catholic and Eastern Orthodox followers believe she is intercessor and mother of the church. She listens to all prayers and acts as intermediary between God and Man.	Hail Mary, full of grace, the Lord is with thee; blessed art thou among women, and blessed is the fruit of thy womb, Jesus. Holy Mary, Mother of God, pray for us... -Amen. Notice that I have taken out the last part of the familiar prayer "Pray for us sinners, now and at the hour of our death." Sin is not a concept supported by this book.
Kuan Yin	In contemporary terms she is seen as the Goddess of Compassion and Mercy. She aslo taught an advanced magnetic kundalini process.	chant the mantra: OM MANI PADME HUM

Table 7-2 Archangels

Name	Background	Methods of Invocation
Michael	(*translation: who is like God*) Performs God's Kindness	"I now invoke the mighty and powerful Archangel Michael to stand at my right-hand side. Please grant me the strength, courage, integrity, and protection I need to fulfill my purpose in this incarnation. Please use your sword to cut away any doubts and negativity. Surround me with your protection, so that I may always work on the side of good. Thank you." [1]
Gabriel	(*translation: The Strength of God*) Performs Acts of Justice and Power	"I now invoke the mighty and powerful Archangel Gabriel to stand behind me. Please bring me insights so that I may always walk in the light. Remove all my doubts and fears, and purify my body, mind, and spirit. Thank you."
Raphael	(*translation: God Heals*) God's healing force	"I now invoke the mighty and powerful Archangel Raphael to stand in front of me. Please fill me with wholeness and good health. Help me heal the wounds from the past. Please heal and restore every aspect of my being. Thank you."[1]
Uriel	(*translation: God is my light*) Leads us to destiny	"I now invoke the mighty and powerful Archangel Uriel to stand on my left-hand side. Please release all my tensions, worries, and insecurities. Grant me tranquility and peace of mind. Help me to serve others, and to give and receive generously. Thank you."[1]

Note: if you are drawn to the idea of angels, you would most likely enjoy working with *Angel Oracle Cards* that allow you to intuitively embrace the wisdom and divine intervention of angels in your day to day challenges.

References

1. http://www.beliefnet.com/Inspiration/Angels/2006/09/Invoking-The-Four-Archangels.aspx

8

What Do We Want? - Unity Consciousness! When Do We Want It? - Now!

There is ultimately only one authentic purpose in Collective Heart Yoga - our *collective* manifestation of Unity Consciousness to heal our planet. Unity Consciousness is the next possible evolutionary leap for humankind. Moreover, the achievement of Unity Consciousness is Creation's diploma for the graduation of Earth's consciousness from a 3-dimensional existence.

Unity Consciousness means that we perceive our reality from a greatly expanded vista that embraces all of Humanity, Mother Earth, and the Heavens. The conflicts in duality will dissipate. Left and right brain will act in balance and harmony. The distance will close between good and bad, male and female, Humanity and God, until we at last see ourselves as manifestations of the Divine as well as divine manifestors.

The concept of *guru* and *disciple* is perfect example of duality that belongs to the Old World. The very idea of worshiping anything other than your own highest nature only gets in the way of the essential message of personal empowerment as a co-creator.

Unity Consciousness is akin to the *noosphere* as described by Teilhard de Chardin and Vladimir Vernadsky, The noosphere is an evolved sphere of life on Earth that encompasses the minds of all individual humans; in essence, our tangible awareness of Jung's collective unconscious. The internet is the digital metaphor of this evolving human connection.

The unifying, energetic influence of Unity Consciousness has also been referred to as the *Christ Consciousness Grid*, which we will learn more about later in this chapter. Dr. Carl Calleman's interpretation of the Mayan calendar best explains why this energetic window of Unity is opening *NOW*.

The Mayan Calendar: A schedule for the evolution of consciousness

In the 1970's a Swedish Biologist, Dr. Carl Calleman, had a mind blowing realization from studying a stone relic called Stele 1 from Coba, Mexico depicting the Maya Long Count Calendar. As Dr. Calleman began to fill in the periods of the calendar with historical content, a pattern emerged that showed marked, predictable surges of evolution in consciousness. He realized that the Mayan Calendar system was far more than a record of the journeys of celestial objects. The Calendar also appears to be a remarkably accurate timetable documenting *and predicting* the journey of *consciousness* from the Big Bang to the Big Unification.

I strongly suggest you read Calleman's *The Mayan Calendar and the Transformation of Consciousness*, and or watch Ian Lungold's engaging lectures on Calleman's work. For the purposes of this text, I'd like to present a brief distillation of the Mayan Long Count Calendar according to Dr. Calleman.

The calendar is best represented as a Mayan Pyramid (*figure 8-2*). This pyramid has nine progressive cycles called underworlds. These underworlds represent quantum leaps in consciousness. Each cycle is divided into seven days and six nights. The length of the underworld's days and nights decrease by a power of 20 as you move up into the next cycle.

Who living on Earth today cannot feel the pace of life accelerating? You can also think of the calendar as showing an exponential acceleration of Creation. On the cusp of the Universal Cycle, the Mayans anticipated it will take us only 18 days to accomplish the same amount of creation or conscious evolution that took 1.26 billion years in the Cellular cycle, and required 20 years in the recent planetary cycle experienced by our parents and grandparents and... yes, even by some of us. The exponential increase in this Universal Cycle is expected to be so rapid, and the time between an intention and its manifestation will soon become so small that the impossible act of co-creation becomes second nature to many.

The Science and Practice of Manifesting Unity Consciousness

Figure 8-2 The Nine Underworlds

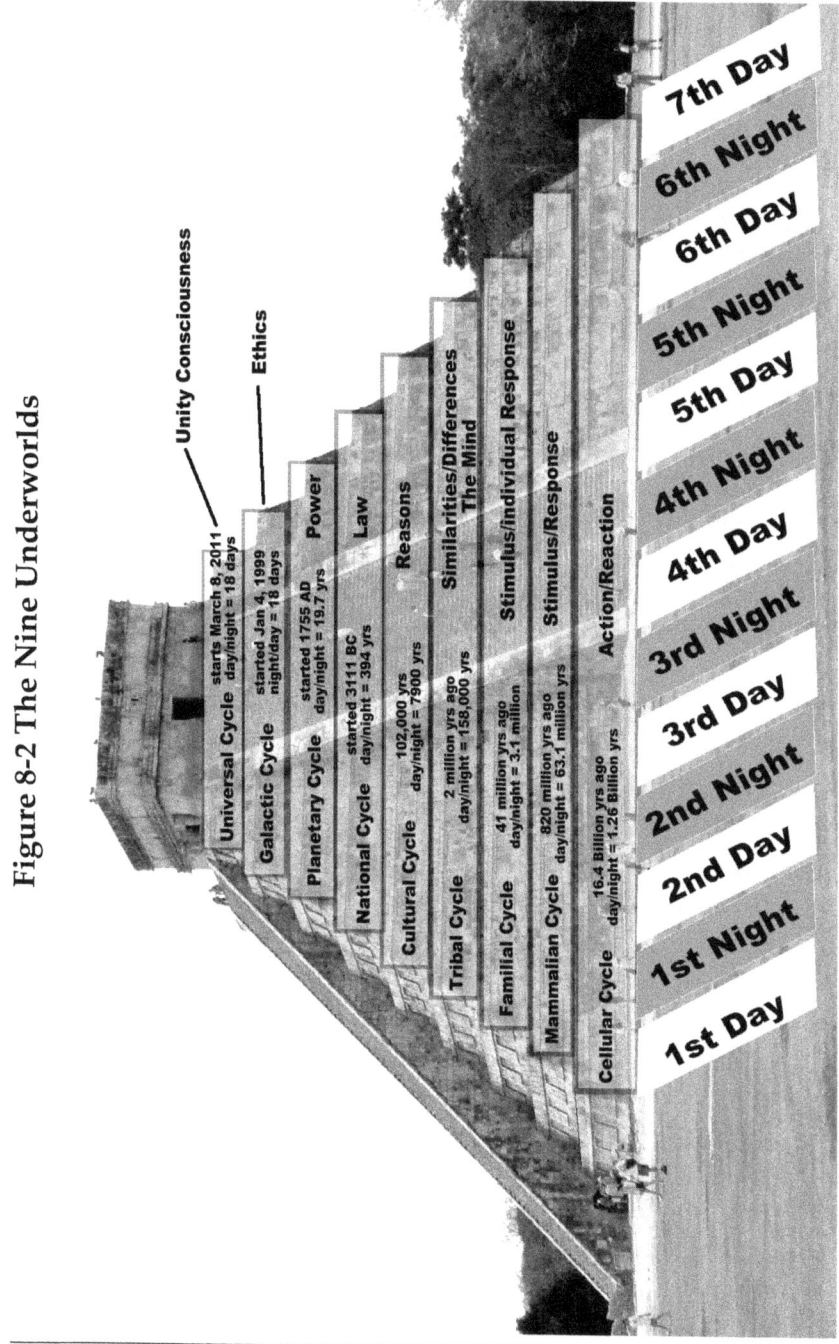

The Cycles of the Mayan Long Count Calendar

Cellular Cycle
- Started over 16.4 billion years ago.
- The Mayans divided 16.4 billion years by 13, or 1.26 billion years for every day and night of the cellular cycle.
- The consciousness expressed in this cycle was one of action/reaction, creating the physical laws of the universe.
- Cells were created toward the end of this cycle.

Mammalian Cycle
- Started 41 million years ago
- Beginning of multicellular organisms
- Evolution of mammals
- 1st live births
- The consciousness expressed in this cycle was one of stimulus/response.

Familial Cycle
- Started 41 million years ago
- The human animal began to employ their brain as a tool.
- Australopithicus, the first tailless ape, thrived in this period.
- The consciousness developed in this cycle was the discrimination of similarities and differences - a further evolution of the power of the mind.
- Rather than just acting and reacting decisions were made

Cultural Cycle
- Started 102,000 years ago.
- Man has developed speech.
- Man imagines reasons for why things happen.
- Cultural groups formed who shared the same reasons for phenomena.

National Cycle
- Started around 3115 BC.
- Humans created writing around the beginning of this cycle.
- Agriculture allowed us to settle down, specialize, and civilize ourselves.
- The consciousness of law or justice evolves out of this cycle.
- Sovereign nations result

Planetary Cycle
- Started in 1755 AD.
- The beginning of the Industrial Revolution.
- The consciousness evolved during this cycle was about advanced production and consolidation of material power and possessions.
- Corporate powers supersede the laws of nations and people.
- Power of life, death, and prosperity held in fewer and fewer hands.

Galactic Cycle
- Started January 4, 1999 AD.
- The consciousness produced from this cycle concerns the development and dispensing of Ethics.
- "Morality"? Rules derived from culture. "Ethics"? The sense of right and wrong we develop from within.
- It's all about integrity here.

Universal Cycle
- Begins on or about February 10, 2011
- The consciousness expressed in this cycle brings us to the unity of all consciousness.
- Because of the ever shortening distance between intention and manifestation, we realize our power of conscious co-creation.

Collective Heart Yoga

Mayan Calendar and the flow of Information

The rise of consciousness expressed in the Long Count can also be understood in terms of the Universe's observable processes for transferring information. And what is consciousness, other than a dynamic of transfering and processing information?

Table 8-1 The Mayan Calendar and the evolution of informational processing and transference.

Cycle	Modes of information storage, processing, and transference
Cellular 16.4 billion years ago	Through the evolution of pure energy, the fundamental consciousness of action and reaction becomes imprinted in matter, from atoms, molecules, proteins, RNA ,DNA. The first life-form emerges as single cells.
Mammalian 41 million years ago	The first mammals appear with brains and nervous systems complex enough to operate with the consciousness of *stimulus and response* which is imprinted in DNA to be passed on to future generations, for the sake of survival.
Familial 41 million years ago	Mammals such as monkeys develop nervous system complex enough for DNA to be imprinted with the consciousness of *stimulus and individual response* rather than a swarming or herding response to stimuli. This level of consciousness, in the form of good and bad individual experiences, is passed on in future generations of animals, for the sake of survival.
Tribal 2 million years ago	The first hominid or tailless, upright apes appear with nervous systems complex enough to use a consciousness of mind that can discriminate similarities and differences. The lessons of these experiences are passed on to future generations via DNA, for the sake of survival.
Cultural 102,000 years ago	Homo Sapiens evolve a nervous system complex enough to activate a consciousness that looks for reasons behind phenomenon, These reasons are passed on to future generations via speech and art and traditions to sustain the survival of cultural forms.

The Science and Practice of Manifesting Unity Consciousness

National Started around 3115 BC	Humans develop writing, which enables a consciousness of law to be passed on to future generations for the survival of nation states. Writing evolves from an artisan's clay cuneiform tablets, to the mechanical printing press informing entire populations.
Planetary Started in 1755 AD	Humans develop the telegraph, radio, telephones, tv, cell phones, and computers, all being modes of communication that allows man to consolidate his dominant power over the planet.
Galactic Started January 4, 1999 AD	The internet becomes a quantum leap in the ability to store, evaluate, and transfer information with more depth connectivity, speed, and mobility. The neural nature of the internet's network allows any individual to communicate with the rest of mankind inexpensively and without the need for intermediaries or institutions who formerly controlled information. This creates a social transparency that inevitably reveals and unravels the web of lies that have enslaved humanity. The consciousness that evolves values integrity.
Universal Begins on or about February 10, 2011	Humanity's technology has created an overwhelming environment of information that changes so rapidly the limited, individual, conscious mind cannot keep up. Humanity's all-consuming obsession with power and the domination of Earth provokes ecological crisis. Humanity is forced to respond to this crisis with a way of sharing information that requires a more evolved consciousness of unity. These new paths of sharing are neurally networked like the brain, and are no longer limited by the intermediary of language, providing profound depths of information, and will allow humanity to communicate collectively between other evolved consciousness. We end our cosmic quarantine and become universal.

Out of time, Out of mind

Are you feeling overwhelmed these days? We've discussed how the acceleration of creation gives us the impression time, itself, is speeding up. Quantum physics has the math to prove it. As the end of the Mayan Long Count Calendar approaches, time will seem to move so fast that, at some point, the limited processing power of the mind will not be able to catch up. The same mind that was evolved over millions of years for humanity's survival will ultimately and inevitably become a detriment to our future survival.

In this current cycle, the average mind is severely stressed. Many of our brothers and sisters choose to *drop out* and *check out* through suicide, alcoholism, drug abuse, television, gaming, the Internet and artificial "communities" like Facebook, World of Warcraft, and Second Life.... opportunities for distraction have never been so abundant. Yet the real solution to this rising crisis of the mind is to give up the mind and trust our intuition. Our intuition is hard-wired to our unconscious which can process far more information than the conscious mind.

Our visual cortex processes reality at 60 frames per second. At the lowest threshold, called the flicker rate (24 frames/sec.), the phenomenon causes a series of still frames to appear animated like real life... hence the name - "motion pictures". Video looks -and feels- very different visually than film because it scans reality at 30 frames per second.

When these limits on the mind disappear so do the artificial constructs that separate us like ethnicity, religion, nationality. It is predictable that some backward-facing minds will cling desperately to whatever once defined them back in the Old World. Yet a much smaller critical mass of souls intending Unity Consciousness can start a chain reaction of conscious evolution which nothing or no one on Earth can stop.

Credible studies suggest it requires only the square root of 1 percent of the world's population to serve as the catalyst for lasting change to occur. If you estimate the Earth's population at 6.6 billion, you would need fewer than 8,200 unified people to alter the destiny all Humanity.

For a comprehensive understanding of this authentic Power of We Few, I recommend a very popular Best Seller:

The Science and Practice of Manifesting Unity Consciousness

The Tipping Point by Malcolm Gladwell. He makes a powerful statistical and scientific case that it takes only three people (together with 160 True Believers) to alter the course of our core culture, society, values and beliefs. Further, he demonstrates how Change is always accomplished simply - through the little things we agree to achieve.

Goodbye causality, Hello co-creation

Due to this acceleration of change, our current construct of time will lose its grip on our consciousness. As time becomes less important, so will the current belief in causality. As mentioned in Chapter 3, *Manifesting in the Eternal Moment*, most of us currently perceive all of reality, including ourselves, as billiard balls in a complex cosmic game of pool. As we approach Unity Consciousness, that pool table universe will inevitably be seen for what it is: an infinite, interconnected system of energy shifting from one frequency to another, having no defined limits or boundaries.

For example, instead of the following paradigm.

A ⟶ B ⟶ C

our reality will simply mirror

ABC

Within this unified system, all things are possible through conscious manifestation. Yet this can only happen when we act from a unified consciousness rather than an illusory, fragmented one. In fact, we have always shared the same consciousness; we have simply been fooled by our false sense of isolated identity. Unity Consciousness will only make apparent what was hidden but always true... Always.

Acoustic Archetypes

In Chapter 6, we discussed the formations which are created when loose sand moves on a metal sheet vibrating with sound waves. When the tone is pure and of certain frequencies, very beautiful symmetric patterns are created. As the frequency increases, more complex geometric patterns are formed. Yet these experiments were essentially producing two-dimensional representations of sound.

Students of Dr. Buckminster Fuller used a balloon dipped in dye and projected pure tones of sound into the balloon. Wherever the vibrations cancelled each other out were areas of no activity called nodes represented on the balloon by collecting spots of dye. There were also faint lines of dye connecting all the nodes as seen in figure 8-2.

Figure 8-2 Negative Image of Buckminster Fuller Balloon Sound Demonstration

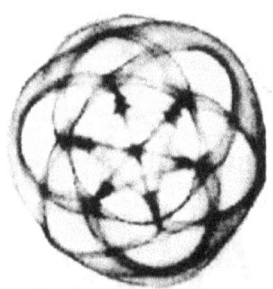

By this simple demonstration, Dr. Fuller and his students proved that sound had a three-dimensional structure. Other geometric structures that fit perfectly into the spherical shape of the balloon are called Platonic solids *(as shown in figure 8-3)*:

Figure 8-3 The Platonic Solids

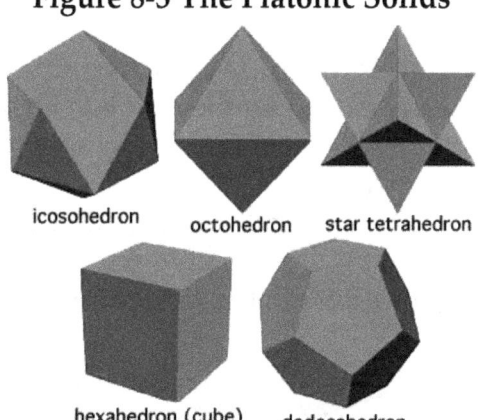

icosohedron   octohedron   star tetrahedron

hexahedron (cube)   dodecahedron

Sound is vibration. So is the rest of creation.

By extrapolation, everything and everyone on Earth has their own geometric grid of vibration that surrounds and permeates each object. Plato believed the Earth had a dodecahedron grid, which penetrates every aspect of existence because it is both fractal and holographic. This grid has been the template in which life-force energy is distributed. It is nothing less than the template of material creation. All atomic particles, atoms, and molecules are organized within the blueprint of the grid. Examine this electron diffraction photograph of the decagonal Al-Co-Ni molecule:

Figure 8-4 Electron Diffraction of decagonal Al-Co-Ni[1]

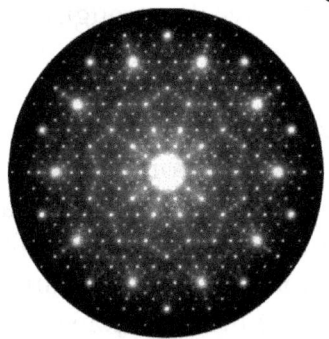

Unity Consciousness as the Christ Consciousness Grid

The age of Earth's own dodecahedron grid is ending or, rather, is being superseded by the next level of the planetary vibrational blueprint: the stellated dodecahedron (as shown in figure 8-5).

Figure 8-5 Stellated Dodecahedron

The dodecehedron represents unconditional love. Yet this structure does not have the strength and stability of structure to persist in 3 dimensions. On rare occasions humans can experience this vibrational state of bliss, but are hard-pressed to carry this energy into the physical world. As time/creation continues to accelerate, the effort becomes more effortless.

The Christ Consciousness grid as a stellated dodecahedron is an infinitely more stable structure. Within this grid, the state of unconditional love is stable and persistent because of the addition of mindfulness or conscious awareness. So, in

The Science and Practice of Manifesting Unity Consciousness

essence, the Christ Consciousness grid represents a state of your conscious awareness of unconditional love. [2]

A representation of the Christ Consciousness Grid surrounding Earth is useful as an object of meditation in Collective Heart Yoga to translate and then to anchor the intent for Unity Consciousness from the conscious to the unconscious mind.

Figure 8-6 Earth's Christ Consciousness Grid

Call to Action

In each of those 9 underworlds, every new wave of consciousness was seeded halfway through the cycle preceding it. In the last few cycles involving humans, there has always been a more evolved contingent of early-adapters providing momentum to rise into the next wave of consciousness. The Renaissance around 1428 AD launched the pre-wave that became our Planetary Cycle starting in 1755 AD. The Harmonic Convergence movement was the pre-wave that gave momentum to the rise of the faster Galactic Cycle starting in 1999 AD.

The window of opportunity for gaining momentum for the rise of Universal Cycle and Unity Consciousness opens July 2010. Dr. Calleman called for a world-wide observance of the Cosmic Convergence July 17-18th, 2010.

I am in agreement with Dr. Calleman that it is absolutely critical that we deliberately choose Unity Consciousness. Otherwise, we will miss the greatest opportunity humanity has ever had for a swift collective evolution. As you read these words, the Earth herself is presently seeking a way to evolve her consciousness, and we are vital components.... instruments....her synapses, so to speak, necessary for this more evolved state. Every level of the Mayan Long Count Calendar can be characterized as an improved capacity for passing information to the future. Our minds, in conjunction with digital informational processing, represent the current apex of Nature's efforts.

Most days, it is my personal belief that we humans are, indeed, the crown jewels of Nature's 4.6 billion-year investment in the evolution of consciousness here on Earth. It is ridiculous to think the Universe would be so random as to destroy us in some epic apocalypse. Yet it is equally naive to think our existence will not be radically altered. The quality of what will come next can only be derived from what has come before. And, so far, every step up the ladder of consciousness has offered more freedom, more opportunities for expression, more latitude for control of our experience.

Every new level of consciousness always contains some less evolved elements of consciousness that came before. In other words, anticipate that we will not be coldly dispensed with but, rather, nearly seamlessly integrated into something....bigger. This something bigger will affect the quality of every individual experience. This something bigger is our Realized Collective Consciousness. This consciousness must be surrendered to, then conscientiously exercised.

Collective Heart Yoga, as outlined in Chapter 9 offers a way to tangibly realize such deeper, more evolved connection... right now. The practice also takes advantage of this deeper connection to exercise our collective will, and thus manifest a more enriching, fulfilling life experience for us all.

However, I leave you with one caveat....WE MUST WANT IT!

References

1. http://www.solid.phys.ethz.ch/ott/staff/beeli/Structural_investigation.html

2. Interview with Ronald L. Holt by Julia Griffin Spirit of Ma'at "Earth Energies", Vol. 3, July 2003.http://www.floweroflife.org/art-ronchristgrid.htm

Calleman, C.J. (2004). The Mayan Calendar and the transformation of consciousness. Rochester, Vermont: Bear and Company.

Gladwell, M. (2000) The tipping point : How little things can make a big difference. Boston : Little, Brown, and Company

The Practice of Collective Heart Yoga

Introduction to The Practice

Collective Heart Yoga merges powerful, ancient Indian Tantra and esoteric Tibetan breathing techniques to scientifically and reliably access and project *kundalini* energy. This is a *non-sexualized* practice that has sacred activism as its focus. Our coherent, collective energy is amplified to send a focused intention for Unity Consciousness to heal the human family and Mother Earth as a whole.

Here is one series of exercises recommended to begin Collective Heart. Be certain this is NOT the ONLY way to activate this energy. Advanced Yoga instructors and enlightened individuals are encouraged to adopt and adapt specific elements in this sequence to better fit your own rhythms and practices, then visit the forum our website at CollectiveHeartYoga.org to post and share your most effective variations and results.

The Science and Practice of Manifesting Unity Consciousness

It is suggested that participants practice the more solitary exercises at home on a daily basis to help open closed energetic channels. Don't be overly concerned if there is some emotional release during private or collective practice. If done within a loving, supportive context such release will always be beneficial. Such commitment to practice will make the group gatherings all the more powerful and more easily facilitated.

Step 1 - Introduction, Namaste Circle, and Inner Smile

As participants enter, place a dab of tiger balm between their eyebrows (with their permission, of course!). The balm will help to open the Ajna or Third Eye, therefore assisting the participant in using *witness consciousness* to feel a sense of separation from emotional drama that could arise during the practice (see page 29 for a more detailed description of *witness consciousness*). In addition to the tiger balm, facilitators will hand out copies of the *Group Unity Decree (pg. 162)*.

Participants will sit in a group circle and introduce themselves to everyone by saying *namaste, my name is John, Mary, etc.* The facilitator will read the Group Unity Decree after everyone has introduced themselves in a group circle. Participants should silently commit to only those aspects of the decree that resound as truth to them. It is important for participants to focus solely on the feelings that the decree evokes for them. This is because only feeling that have the vibration high enough to communicate intent to the Universe.

While still seated in the circle, participants will close their eyes and follow along as the facilitator guides them in the following inner-smile meditation.

It is absolutely critical for each participant to achieve what's referred to in energetic arts, as the *inner smile*. The inner smile is different from an *outer smile* because the outer smile is directed at something or someone external, while the inner smile is directed internally, therefore always coming from a place that's pure and authentic, much like the famous smile of the Mona Lisa or Dalai Lama, for instance.

Figure 9-1 Famous Inner Smiles

In yogic terms, the inner smile pulls muscles in the back of the neck away from the center of the medulla to open what is called the mouth of God, an energetic gate that permits energy into and out of the inner eye, as shown in figure 9-2.

Figure 9-2 Inner Smile Anatomy

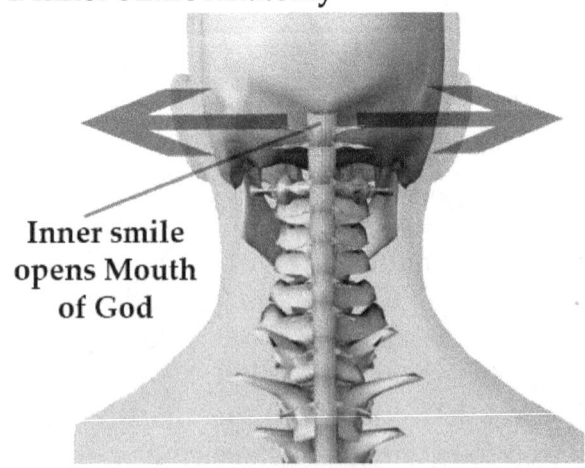

The Science and Practice of Manifesting Unity Consciousness

Inner smiles have the following characteristics:
- Loosen stuck energy
- Harmonize underlying tensions
- Are directed inward
- Are an external sign of loving yourself from within
- Integrates body reality with soul reality
- Arises from the 3 brains (mind brain, heart brain, gut brain)

Inner Smile Meditation

The following inner smile meditation is adapted from a Doaist methodology which considers the inner smile to be a yin or water method which produces an inner alchemy if performed with proper precision and intent.

1. Imagine a golden egg of light above your head
2. Smile into this golden egg of light
3. Visualize this golden egg releasing light that diffuses into the brain.
4. Smile into the left brain, smile into the right brain, then smile into the middle of the brain. Internally love your brain while you are smiling.
5. Smile into your eyes. From your eyes smile into the lower brain then down into the entire spinal cord. Let the golden egg of light release its light into the entire spinal cord. Internally love your spinal cord
6. Visualize the light from the golden egg entering your crown and traveling down your spine to your heart. Smile into your heart
7. Gather saliva into your mouth. Imagine the light from the golden egg above your head infusing your saliva with golden light. Roll the saliva around the mouth with your tongue for a while. Now squeeze the neck muscles as much as comfortably possible. Swallow the saliva in one gulp. Imagine the golden liquid warming and infusing the

following in sequence: the esophagus, stomach, small intestines, large intestine, colon, and finally root. Watch everything turn warm with golden light. Smile into every organ as the golden saliva goes down your digestive track.

Step 2 - Energizing the Body

Music body shake (3-4 minutes) - The purpose of the Music body shake is to energize the body. After a brisk period of enthusiastic shaking participants should be more in tune with their subtle energies. Such energetic sensitivity will be very useful during the rest of the practice.
- Start playing music with a primal, strong dancing beat.
- Lead Participants to shake feet first, then legs, hips, arms and head.
- Stop the music abruptly and ask participants to freeze. Ask them to feel which parts of their body are not vibrating with energy. Encourage them to focus on that part of their body as they continue to dance. Resume music.

Soulful Energetic Dance (3-4 minutes)
- Have everyone put on a blindfold. Instruct participants to start dancing in a slow graceful manner - as if they were doing T'ai Chí, feeling their own energy, then extending to sense the energy of others.
- Start playing soulful, slow tantric-type music. Facilitators should look out for possible, although rare, collisions between participants.
- After music finishes, have participants take off blindfolds. Ask them to stand at least arm's length apart from each other to prepare for *Karana Kriyas* or *T'ai Chí Ruler*.

Step 3 - Aligning the Meridians

Karana Kriyas

These exercises, know by some as Rishi Isometrics,

The Science and Practice of Manifesting Unity Consciousness

were developed by Rishis, holy men in the Himalayas. The power of these kriyas is the use of dynamic tension. I chose these exercises because of their simplicity and effectiveness at aligning the meridians and energizing the body. When performing the *Karana Kriyas* it is best to engage every muscle possible with slow, graceful, deliberate movements. Spread feet at hip's width. Always inhale through the nose and exhale through the mouth to energize the body. Perform each exercise 7 times. [1]

1. Reaching the sky - this exercise opens the front of the lungs

Figure 9-3 Reaching The Sky

1. Stand with arms at your side, then slowly raise your arms above your head while pressing your hands together in dynamic tension for about 3 seconds. As you are raising your arms, inhale and raise onto your "tippy toes."
2. Lower arms slowly to your waist as you exhale and lower the soles of your feet firmly to the floor.

2. Reach the sky reversing palms of the hand - This exercise opens the backs of the lungs.
- Basically repeat the normal Reaching the Sky exercise, except press the back of the palms together rather than the front of the palms.

3. Side Bend

1. As you inhale, raise your arms above your head and interlock the thumbs together in dynamic tension.
2. As you exhale, bend to the left side while continuing to hold dynamic tension between your thumbs and maintaining your elbows on the same plane as your head. When you have bent down as far as you can go on your left side, hold the tension for 3 seconds, feeling the channels of energy opening all the way from the edge of your right foot, up your right leg, right side of your abdomen, right side of your chest and, finally, along the right side of your neck.
3. With arms still in position, inhale and return back to full standing position with arms still above the head and thumbs interlocking in sustained dynamic tension.
4. Reverse thumb positions and repeat to the right side.
5. Repeat this set seven (7) times each on the right and left sides. Make sure to change position of the thumbs when bending to the opposite side.
6. Lower your arms slowly and feel the energy coursing through your body. Enjoy the moment.

Figure 9-4 Side Bends

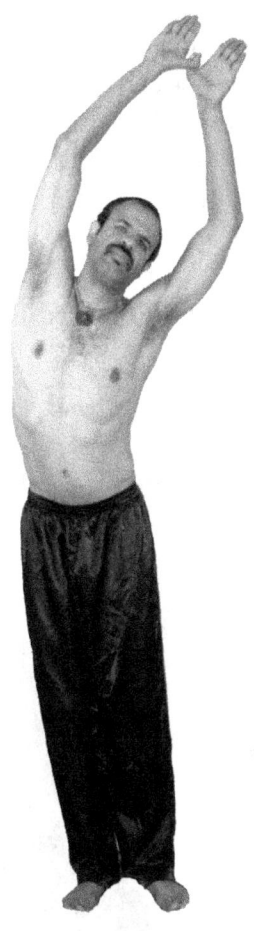

4. Forward Bend
1. Interlock thumbs behind your back with dynamic tension and step forward with your left foot.
2. Keep the chin up to open the *Jalandhara banda (The energetic gate located in your neck)* as you slowly bend forward, lifting both arms behind your back while you exhale. Feel the dynamic tension open an energetic channel from your

sacrum up your back, to your medulla.
3. While you inhale, return to a full standing position, lowering your arms back down to your buttocks, thumbs still interlocked in dynamic tension.
4. Repeat this exercise seven (7) times with left foot forward, and seven more with right foot forward. (Feel free to experiment / It is recommended) to alternate left-right, but can also complete a series of seven to one side before switching polarity.

Figure 9-5 Forward Bends

The Science and Practice of Manifesting Unity Consciousness

5. Back Bend

- Stand with heels together. While you inhale. raise hands above the head, palms together employing dynamic tension. Bend backward as far as you can comfortably go.
- Then slowly exhale while bending over. Keep arms extended above head until arms, head, and torso are parallel to the floor.

Figure 9-6 Back Bends

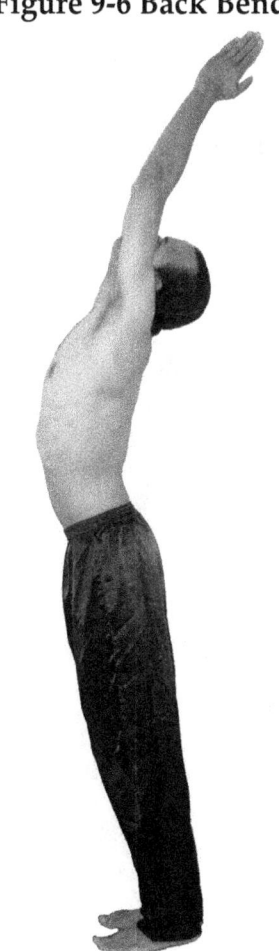

Collective Heart Yoga

- Repeat seven (7) times. At the last exhalation bending forward, let go of your arms and head to hang loose, like a rag doll. You should feel energy coursing up your back.

6. Twist
- While standing in a balanced position, inhale and twist body to the left, raising the right palm to the sky and the lowering the left palm to the Earth... stretch with tension.
- Inhale and untwist the body slowly, and bring both hands in front of you to waist level with palms facing each other.
- Repeat seven (7) times, alternately twisting to the right and left side.

Figure 9-7 Twists

The Science and Practice of Manifesting Unity Consciousness

T'ai Chi Ruler or Immortals Wand

This very simple exercise was attributed to a Taoist recluse, Chen Hsi-I, over 1000 years ago. Chen taught the system to an emperor of the Sung Dynasty, who considered the practice so powerful that it was kept secret from the masses and was only made available to the West in the 1970's.

The wand is a 10.5 to 11 inch wooden dowel of specific design which strengthens the immune system by stimulating a vital point in the palms. It also creates a circuit for vital energies to flow effortlessly through specific meridians of the body.

When performing the practice it is important to maintain the following conditions.

- Breathing should be slow, inhaling though the nose and exhaling through the mouth.
- The tongue should touch the roof of the mouth. Yoga refers to this as *Kechari Mudra*. This connects the *Governer's Channel* to the *Conception Vessel,* a circuit flowing up the spine over the head and circling back down over the front of the body which flows up and down the spine and head.
- The wand should be held lightly between the palms with the tip of each index finger touching the thumbs.
- Concentrate your attention on the bead in the middle of the wand while performing the exercises.
- Slightly tip your tailbone forward. Keep the back straight, rolling your shoulders forward.
- Keep your knees so that you can no longer see your feet.
- Move the wand slowly as if you are moving through thick honey. The slow movements enhance the pull of Shakti energy from the Earth and Cosmic or Shiva energy from the sky into the body.

Grounding - Stand with feet at hips' width. Hold the wand at navel level. Be aware of the connection to the Earth. All wand movements will begin and end at this state.

Forward Circles - Holding the wand at navel level slowly lift the wand above the head as you inhale and exhale as you lower the wand. Inhale as you lift the wand / Exhale as you lower the wand. Then reverse direction of the wand.

Rocking Side Circles - step the left foot out at a 45 degree angle. With the body facing the extended foot slowly rotate the wand inhaling while lifting from the navel center and exhaling while lowering the wand. As you lift the wand rock the heel of the foot lifting the toes. With the toes firmly implanted lift the heel while lowering the wand.

Figure 9-8 Rocking side circles

The Science and Practice of Manifesting Unity Consciousness

Torque - Hold the wand at navel level with the right hand on the top and the left hand on the bottom. Exhale while you laterally move the wand to you left. At the end of the movement to the left, flip the wand so that the left hand is now on top. Inhale as you bring the wand back to the center at navel level. Then with the left hand still on top, exhale while laterally moving the wand as far as you can to the right. At the end of movement to the right, flip the wand so that the right hand is now on top then inhale while bringing the wand back to center position at navel level.

Figure 9-9 Torque

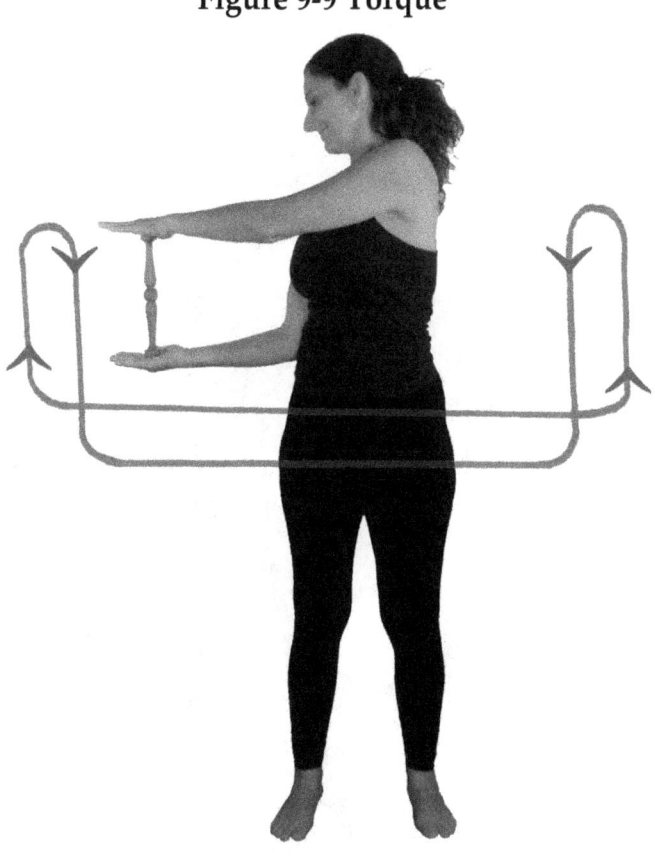

Twist and Bend - Step your left foot out at a 45 degree angle. While facing the extended foot slowly lift the wand from the navel position, inhaling as you lift the wand. Exhale as you lower the wand, bending your back so that you are practically touching your extended toe with the wand. Then, all in one continuous movement, inhale while lifting the wand to navel level. Reverse the direction of the wand. Then repeat the above sequence with the right foot extended.

Figure 9-10 Bend and twist

Lift - As you inhale, lift onto the balls of your feet as you raise the wand above your head from navel level. Exhale and lower to the soles of your feet as you lower the wand. Lifting on to the balls of your feet will stimulate what's called the *bubbling springs* which is the entry point in the body for Shakti energy from the Earth.[4]

Figure 9-11 Lifts

Step 4 - Stimulating the Anahata (Heart Chakra)

Below are some exercises that will help participants tune into the vibration of their Anahata or heart chakra. It is sufficient to only perform one of these exercises before advancing to the Tibetan Seed Mantras. I personally find the Roving Heart Beat to be more interactive in a group setting.

Anahata - Bhramari Pranayama (Humming Bee Breath)

The Humming Bee Breath will help to open the heart chakra. It is important for participants to really feel the vibration of their humming.

Figure 9-12 Bhramari Pranayama

The Science and Practice of Manifesting Unity Consciousness

1. Sit in meditative posture, eyes closed with back and neck straight.
2. Put index fingers in both ears.
3. Inhale deeply.
4. As you exhale slowly, *hum*. It is not important that the humming is loud or in any particular key.
5. While humming, adjust your pitch and tone so you can feel the resonant vibration in your head. Do not strain during any part of this exercise. Perform for at least 10min.

Roving Heart Beat

     This is an exersise that came to me in meditation. Often times the heart cannot be adequately accessed because of issues of control which are rooted in the third chakra. The Roving Heart Beat connects the heart chakra with the manipura or third chakra. The roving about the room allows participants to actively visualize both the giving and recieving of heart energy.

- While in standing position, cross arms over the chest so that the right palm is over the upper left side of the chest and the left palm is over the upper right side of the chest.
- Slowly beat the right palm onto the left side of the chest and slide it down past your solar plexus.
- Slowly beat the left palm onto the right side of the chest and slide it down.
- Alternate the beating and sliding of each palm at comfortable pace - speeding up and slowing down at will.
- While alternately beating the palms on the chest repeatedly voice the mantra, SA, in a low but sharp voice.
- Close the eyes so that you can barely see the ground ahead of you and slowly walk across the room allowing your energy to guide you toward and away from other

participants in the room. Visualize green love energy emanating from the heart and connecting with others in the room. Be sure to engage the inner-smile.

Step 5 - Sounding of the Chakras

The following exercises use Tibetan Seed Mantras, which, if done correctly, are very powerful. It is possible to get a head rush the first few times performing this exercise, *so take it easy.*

- Muladhara: Place the opposite hand over the genitals, visualize a spinning red energy penetrating the front of the body, and exiting through the back. Take in a deep breath and chant LAM.
- Swadhisthana: Place the opposite hand slightly below the navel, visualize spinning orange energy penetrating the front of the body, and exiting through the back. Take in a deep breath and chant VAM.
- Manipura: Place the opposite hand over the solar plexus/ sternum, visualize spinning yellow energy penetrating the front of the body, and exiting through the back. Take in a deep breath and chant RAM.
- Anahata: Place the opposite hand over your heart, visualize spinning green energy penetrating the front of the body and exiting through back. Take in a deep breath and chant YAM repeatedly until running out of breath. Perform at least 4 breaths of Yam repititions.
- Ajna: Place one hand over the third eye - one finger width above the eye brows. Visualize spinning indigo energy penetrating from the front of the forehead, going through your brain and leaving out the back of the head. Take in a deep breath and exhale while chanting OM.
- Visuddhi: Place opposite hand over the throat, visualize spinning sky blue energy penetrating the front of the

body, and exiting through the back. Take in a deep breath and chant HAM.
- Sahasrara: Lightly tap the top of the head with the fingertips continuously for about two 2 minutes. This will help open the Crown Chakra. Then, sitting quietly, internalize the mantra OM again and again at a slow even pace, keeping the attention on the area right above the crown of the head.

Begin going up spine and then repeat the steps going down the spine. This should be done three times. There should be tingling sensations in the body and palms.[2]

The Tibetan Seed Mantras can be enhanced with the addition of Lawrence Buchine's *Chakra Chromatics* developed from a profound understanding of the mathematical patterns contained in the Kabbalah's Tree of Life.. Essentially it is performing the same same toning steps as described above with the addition of hearing Buchine's sustained musical notes (Table 9-1) while sounding the seed mantras and visualizing the corresponding chakra colors.

Table 9-1 Buchine's Chakra Chromatics

Musical Note	Chakra	Frequency
Middle C	Muladdhara (1st)	261.6Hz
D above middle C	Swadistana (2nd)	293.7Hz
E above middle C	Manipura (3rd)	312.6Hz
F above middle C	Anahata (4th)	349.2Hz
G above middle C	Vishuddi	392Hz
A above middle C	Ajna	440Hz
B above middle C	Sahasrara	493.9Hz

Step 6 - *Calming the Mind*

Nadi Shadhona

Nadi Shadhona is a yogic practice that equalizes the energies of the ida and pingala channel that weave around the shushuma, the central channel of energy along the spinal cord. When the ida and pingala are equalized the shushuma becomes an open channel for energy flow. Performing this exercise before *Step 6 - Exploring the Sacred Heart Space* will greatly enhance the meditative experience of participants by synchronizing left and right hemispheres of the brain, thereby calming the mind. Participants will sit in a circle while performing this exercise.

- Place tip of index finger between and slightly above your eyebrows.
- Use the thumb and the 2nd (middle) finger of the hand to alternately close the right and left nostril.
- Close right nostril with thumb and inhale through the left nostril
- Release thumb from right nostril and use the 2nd finger to close the left nostril.
- Exhale through the right nostril
- With fingers maintaining the same position, inhale through right nostril.
- Close right nostril with thumb, release left nostril with middle finger and exhale through left nostril.
- Repeat all steps for at least five (5) minutes.

Transition Info - Participants will already be seated in easy pose after the conclusion of Nadi Shadhona. This would be a great time for a bathroom break before the heart meditations begin.

Figure 9-13 The Nadis

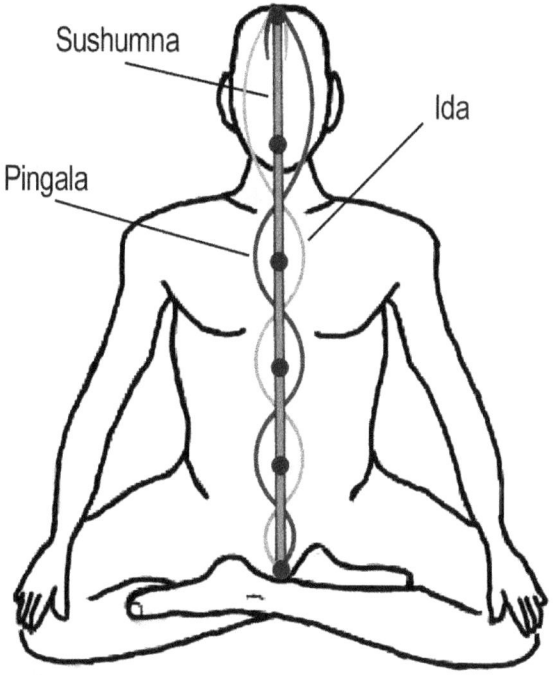

Step 7 - Exploring the Heart Sacred Space Meditation

The first part of the meditation is called the Unity Breath. This breath is important because it unifies the loving presence of the Cosmic Father and Mother Earth in the heart, the Shiva-Shakti Energy which allows you to tangibly become the beloved Cosmic Child, thus completing the Holy Trinity, one of the most fundamental archetypes of our Collective Unconscious.

1. Imagine your most beloved place in nature. Feel the loving and nourishing presence of Mother Earth. Imagine the smell of rich soil, feel the caressing breezes across your face. Feel completely at one with your surroundings. Feel nothing but pure love for Mother Earth and direct this

feeling to flow naturally throughout your entire body.
2. Feel the presence of someone in your life who represents a nurturing mother figure. It is appropriate if it is not the mother who raised you. Feel the caring, unbounded love that only a mother can have for a child.
3. When you are completely filled with maternal loving bliss, allow this love to coalesce in your body as a golden glowing sphere of light. Release this light and let in travel down your spine into the ground and then deep into the Earth. Hold the space; wait patiently for this love to be returned to you. It will come when your love for Mother Earth is, indeed, heartfelt and sincere.
4. Whenever the love of Mother Earth comes to you, permit your self to receive this love *unconditionally*. Do not try to direct it in any way. This is an exercise in surrendering. Just FEEL it.
5. When you feel ready, begin to focus on the sky. Even indoors, you can readily imagine the vastness of the heavens, the Sun, the planets, the Milky Way, other galaxies, and the entire universe. Feel the wise, loving presence of masculine Father Sky.
6. Feel the presence of any nurturing father figure in your life. Feel His unconditional love, the wise hand of guidance and protection. Take comfort. Know that you will want for nothing. Your father will provide everything.
7. When you are ready, allow this love for the paternal to coalesce in the heart as a golden, glowing sphere of light. Hold it, then release this light and allow it to rise from your heart, up your spine, and out from the top of your head into the Heavens. Wait patiently for Father Sky to return this love to you.
8. You will become aware you are now a unified part of the cosmic, holy trinity of Mother, Father, and Child. Bask in this sacred moment. Feel the presence of God pervasive in everything.

Entering the Heart Meditaion

The second part of this key meditation is finding your way into your Heart. Typically, there is a Male Path which *visualizes* that whirling vortex of energy that envelopes the heart. There is also a Female Path which relies more upon instinct and intuition. It doesn't matter which Path you follow, regardless of your actual gender.

The Male Path

1. Imagine your consciousness inside your skull. Feel what it is like inside the confines of that space, with the dome of hard bone surrounding your Mind.
2. Then move your consciousness down into your throat and feel the softness of the flesh, the fragile structure of your windpipe. Visualize yourself with your consciousness standing on the highest Olympics diving platform.
3. When you are ready, jump from the platform and fall into a powerful whirlpool that represents the toroidal field of energy flowing into your Heart (as shown figure 9-8).
4. Your toroidal field is either spinning clockwise or counter clockwise. The direction is less significant than your awareness of it. Just pay attention to how you feel and you will go with the flow. Let yourself - your consciousness - fall into this whirlpool of energy, like a leaf in a swirling water spout. Imagine spinning faster and faster as you get closer to the center of the spout. Imagine yourself falling and falling until you spiral to complete stillness. Remain there for a timeless Moment.

The Female Path

1. If you prefer the female path, imagine your consciousness in your throat passing through the membrane of your

heart into its warm depths. If it is dark within, *command* that there be light.
2. You may hear a vibration, a sound that permeates your heart space. Listen for a while. When you feel ready, begin to softly hum this vibration. Try to duplicate the sound as closely as possible, and keep humming throughout the rest of the exercise.
3. Look around your heart space for a faint green glow. Follow that glow until you come to a large chest. Open this chest and you will see a brilliant, glowing, deep-green emerald. This is the very sacred symbol of your heart. Imagine yourself merging with the radiant emerald to *become* the sacred space of your heart.
4. Stop humming and remain very quiet. You will probably hear a higher pitched vibration now. Try to softly duplicate this vibration with a renewed hum. Remember the specific pitch of this hum, for it is your way to return directly to this place *anytime you wish.* [3]

Figure 9-14 Heart's Toriodal Field

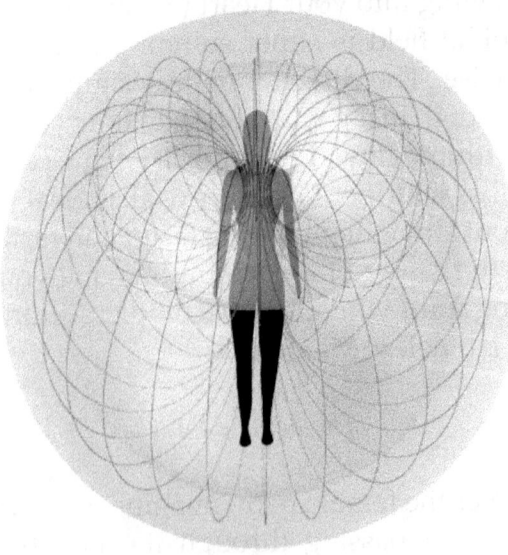

Abundance - an addendum to this meditation

If you care to go further with this particular meditation and internalize even more overflowing abundance, you can follow along through this next optional section.

- As you are continue to hum the vibration of your heart's sacred space, imagine the most beautiful, pristine lake in the world on an absolutely perfect Fall or Spring day.
- Imagine a child picking up an emerald that embodies the sacred space of your heart. Visualize that child throwing the emerald far out into the middle of this deep, tranquil lake. Allow your consciousness to follow - flying, falling, dropping down deep to the bottom of the lake. Feel your heart's vibrant green light illuminating the watery depths.
- Now picture thousands of people surrounding the lake. Every person carries empty bottles, pots, or jugs. See them bending down to gather water to drink. This water is infused and enriched with the emerald light from your Heart's most sacred love.
- An underground spring will replenish you with an infinite supply regardless of how many drink from your lake. The Love in your Heart will never run dry. This represents the true nature of your abundance.

Step 8 - Awakening Awareness of the Collective

Eye Gazing

The following eye-gazing exercise is unparalleled in its ability to facilitate awareness of the collective. It is expected to be a bit uncomfortable for many. However, there will be individuals who are *extremely* uncomfortable with gazing into someone else's eyes for a sustained time. Most often they are very afraid to look within themselves. They are often heavily burdened with karmic residue

Collective Heart Yoga

that has never seen the light of personal awareness.

Facilitators should pay close attention to any participants who are extremely uncomfortable during this exercise. It is wise to encourage an environment of non-judgment. Make it clear that it is perfectly OK to opt out of the practice at any point. However, it is also important to emphasize that each step of the practice must be completed before proceeding to the next. Participants who cannot handle the eye gazing may experience an uncomfortable release of pent up emotions during the powerful Emanating Heart and Manifestation Cobra Breaths.

Participants will make two lines facing each other. Try to have each opposing lines of participants directly facing the other as shown in figure 9-9. If there is an uneven number of participants have the odd man out stand on the side perpendicular to both lines of participants. Rotate every 3 minutes.

Figure 9-15 Eye gazing rotation

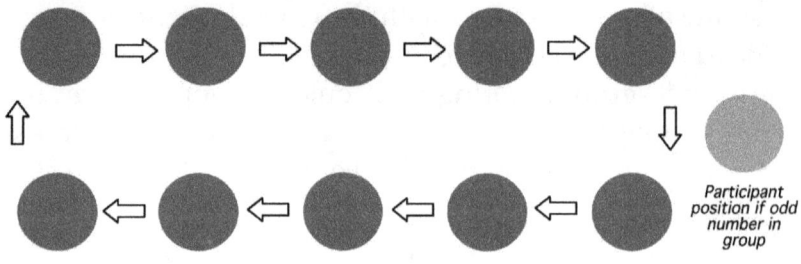

Participant position if odd number in group

Step 9 - *Collective* projection of love and intention for Unity Consciousness

While participants take a quick break, play a music track that can be freely downloaded at CollectiveHeartYoga.org. This track emphasizes 3 distinct beats at a carefully chosen interval that corresponds to the sequence of breaths in the Emanating Heart and the Manifestation Cobra. The 3rd beat

The Science and Practice of Manifesting Unity Consciousness

of the track will have either the mantra, AH for the Emanating Heart Cobra or the mantra, AUM, for the Manifestation Cobra. This rhythm of breath synchronizes the nervous systems of all participants, as well as entrains individual minds to become coherent with the group's consciousness.

When participants return from the break have them gather into duos - ideally males paired with females - sitting back-to-back in meditative position. *(see Appendix A for chart of optional pairing configurations)* Collective Heart Yoga facilitators will now teach participants the *Emanating Heart Cobra Breath* and guide the group toward Unity Consciousness. There is a video animation of both the Emanating Heart and Manifestation Cobra Breaths on the CHY website.

The first thing to convey to participants is what I call the "Hierarchy of Densities in Consciousness," meaning that all reality is some form of consciousness whether it be matter, energy, or thought. The denser or more complex the manifestation of consciousness, the more influence it has on forms of consciousness less complex or dense; hence, the importance of visualization in the practice of CHY. So the following is always true when practicing any type of yoga:

Thought *controls* **Energy** *controls* **Body**

Emanating Heart Cobra Breath

1. Sit in meditative pose.
2. Imagine the infinite wisdom and unconditional love of Father Sky. Picture the vastness of the heavens as you contemplate the nurturing, protective love given to you by a true Father Figure in your life.
3. As you inhale, bring the tip of your tongue to the roof of your mouth or back of your throat, whichever channels

Collective Heart Yoga

the most energy. Imagine the golden light of Father Sky being pulled into your crown. As this energy is pulled into your body, internalize the *earliest* name you gave to your father (*Daddy, Papa, Da-Da*) to establish that connection with your Inner Child.

4. While you are doing all of this, close your Mooladhara or Root Chakra half-way. For women, your root is activated by squeezing the cervix and vaginal muscles behind the cervix where the uterus projects into the vagina (popularly know among women as *kegel* exercises). For men, your root is activated by squeezing the perineal muscles between anus and scrotum.
5. Continue to inhale the golden energy from Father Sky, entering through your crown and now collecting in your heart. See your heart glowing with this golden energy.
6. During the second half of your inhale, squeeze the remaining half of your root and imagine pulling the golden love energy of Mother Earth up into your root, up your spine, and collecting in your heart. As you pull Her energy upwards, internalize the earliest name you gave to your mother (Ma, Ma Ma, Mommy).
7. **[If practicing solo]** Slowly release your Root and voice the mantra AH while mentally projecting the golden/green energy of your heart to the heart of some you love. It is best to visualize looking in the eyes of this person while you project. After you have felt the heart connection of a loved one, the rest of your practice should be focused on people that you don't have an open heart toward.
8. **[if practicing with a collective]** Slowly release your Root and voice the mantra, *AH*, simultaneously allowing the golden/green energy to emanate from your heart throughout the room in waves, like ripples through a pond.

The Science and Practice of Manifesting Unity Consciousness

After the group has learned the Emanating Heart Cobra Breath, the Facilitator will then immediately offer the *Manifesting Heart* Cobra Breath. The significant difference is during exhalation. Instead of *emanating* energy from the heart in ripples, your heart light is released up the spine, through the neck, out through the Crown Chakra and on into the heavens. Together, they prepare and deliver your Intention to the Universe.

Facilitator script for collective intention during Emanating Heart Cobra Breath

Look deep within your heart and determine who is your personal connection to the divine. They can be avatars, like Babaji or Jesus; Saints, such as Mother Mary or St. Peter; or Angels, such as Michael or Gabriel. Ask them to help you to focus on and feel the scenarios that follow.

Visualize and feel your golden love light emanating outward from your heart in like ripple on a pond yet with power of waves from the ocean. See and feel this golden light mixing with the lights of everyone else in the room to produce an exponentially powerful collective golden love light that ripples out from the group in very strong waves that eventually engulf the entire Earth in love. Feel the Earth and its inhabitants changing because of this love. Feel hearts everywhere opening, ready to evolve.

Manifesting Cobra Breath

It is appropriate that the facilitator repeat the identical instructions as above, for the sake of the familiar rhythm, adding emphasis to the dynamic shift at the end which distinguishes *Emanating Heart* from *Manifesting Heart* Cobra Breath.

1. Sit in meditative pose and ask your personal connection to the Divine (See Chapter 7) to fill you with healing light and to help you to effortlessly channel that healing light to the world.
2. Imagine the infinite wisdom and unconditional love of Father Sky. Picture the vastness of the heavens as you contemplate a true Father Figure.
3. As you inhale, bring the tip of your tongue to the roof of your mouth or back of your throat, to channel maximum energy. Imagine the golden light of Father Sky being pulled into your crown. As you inhale internalize the *earliest* name you gave to your father (*Daddy, Papa, Da-Da*) to establish that connection with your Inner Child. As you are doing all of this, again *squeeze* your root half-way closed.
4. Imagine the golden energy inhaled from Father Sky entering your crown, collecting in your heart. Witness your heart glowing bright gold.
5. In the second half of your inhale, again squeeze your Root completely to pull up the golden love energy of Mother Earth into your heart. As you draw Her energy upwards, internalize the earliest name you gave to your mother (Ma, Ma Ma, Mommy).
6. Release your root, now externalizing the mantra, AUM, simultaneously allowing the golden energy to rise from your heart, up the spine, through the neck, and out through the Crown Chakra and into the heavens. Visualize your intention being sent to the Universe as a fount of heart-light.

The Science and Practice of Manifesting Unity Consciousness

Facilitator script for collective intention during Manifestation Cobra Breath

Look deep within your heart and determine who would be your personal connection to the divine. They can be avatars, like Babaji or Jesus; Saints, such as Mother Mary or St. Peter; or Angels such as Michael or Gabriel. Ask them to help you to focus on and feel the scenarios that follow.

Visualize the golden love light of your heart rising from your crown and then mixing with the lights of everyone else in the room to produce an exponentially powerful collective golden love light that rises to the cosmos. Carried with this light is the intention for all life on Earth to unite in consciousness. Feel the love of one-ness, where the illusionary veil of separateness is lifted and all life coexists for the sake of conscious evolution.

Note: This can also be an opportunity to facilitate a collective intention for more specific healing, like peace in a war-torn country or loving open hearts of leaders during times of crisis, for instance. It is important, however, for the facilitator to have the collective's focus completely on visualizing and feeling what the healed scenario would be like as if it were already present.

Group Unity Decree

After reading the above script, the facilitator tells the collective that he/she will read Group Unity Decree *(next page)* adapted from the author, channel, and energy worker, Lisa Renee.[6] The facilitator will ask participants to silently commit themselves to only aspects of the vow that resounds deeply within them. The decree serves as both an intention and commitment of the collective. Remember the criteria for heart-based healing, page 65.

Group Unity Decree

We understand that our true nature is pure consciousness enduring and ever-evolving. We are open to connecting with a larger collective consciousness. We give up nothing and gain more than we can fathom.

From this collective heart space we intend that the entire planet and all its inhabitants connect in heart and consciousness.

We are also open to connecting with more evolved consciousness, terrestrial or extraterrestrial, this dimension or another, as long as they seek light and oneness.

We are ready to evolve now. We are ready to accept the full activation of our DNA. We are ready to unlearn all the lies that have enslaved us. We fully embrace our true power as a multidimensional being. We are ready to love unconditionally.

Thank God... We are the Cosmic Christ.

And so It is, Lovingly Decreed.[6]

Ending the Collective Heart Yoga session

If you are experienced with energetics you can anticipate a sublime state connecting everyone in the room. Their consciousness will have expanded to encompass the collective, if not all Creation. It is important to not abruptly break their entrainment sustained by the drumbeat and resonant mantra. The members of the collectives will experience a synchronization of their nervous systems so many will find it dif-

The Science and Practice of Manifesting Unity Consciousness

ficult to separate from the sacred geometric formation after the mediation is finished. I suggest slowly transitioning to a second instrumental with a comparably slow heartbeat beginning, but evolving to a fast and energetic ending. The energy of the music will take everyone out of entrainment smoothly and gracefully.

Before they leave, new participants might be given a small (3" X 5") image of the Earth surrounded by a glowing, golden stellated dodecehedron, the geometric representation of Unity Christ Consciousness. This image is to be used as an altar object of meditation to translate and anchor your continued intent for this Collective Heart Unity to awaken and unite our conscious, unconscious, and collective unconscious.

Additional instructions for facilitators

- During the group orchestration of the Manifesting Heart Cobra, the facilitator will guide everyone through a visualization of how it feels to be in Unity Consciousness.
- It is important that the facilitator exclude all euphemisms, deities, and specific cultural references, and instead speak at this time in terms of basic human feelings, using archetypal symbology like *Father*, *Mother*, and *Cosmic Child* to connect to the collective unconscious.
- Participants will also be asked to silently summon their own *personal connection to the Divine* or *Divine Emissary* by name (see Chapter 7) to assist them during manifestation of Unity Consciousness.
- With the external mantras during both Cobra breaths, it is critical that participants surrender ownership of their own individual mantras by either raising or lowering their vocal pitch to find resonance with the group as a whole. This surrendering can happen only if the individual participants can recognize when their overall group sound has achieved harmony and discern whether their own particular voice is

adding to (or detracting from) that harmonious resonance.

Equality of presence

The underlying goal of CHY is to create an energetic context where individual hearts integrate facilitating the experience of a unified consciousness. From this unified consciousness a unified intention is projected to the rest of the planet to benefit from that same experience. Therefore it would be counterproductive in the practice of CHY to allow any dynamic that perpetuates the divisiveness of the *Old World*.

One such fragmenting dynamic is the *guru/student* relationship. When I say *guru* I'm referring to any type of teacher supposedly in a position of spiritual elevation. Gurus have served their purpose historically. However, the idea of spiritual elevation has always been an illusion. All souls are enlightened, all souls are of a single consciousness. Some are liberated by this awareness, many are not.

Our current world is one of overwhelming, exponential conscious evolution that ultimately leads to humanity reaching a more highly evolved paradigm in consciousness. That new paridigm is that of an *aware collective consciousness*. All current yoga practices must accomodate participants who are rapidly evolving because of these times. Part and parcel of one's evolution today is gaining personal spiritual insights without an external teacher. The historical guru or external teacher most often symbolizes a destination that is outside the student. As a consequence, the focus of the student is projected outward rather than inward towards the *inner guru* or *higher self*.

The vast majority of those procliamed gurus have egos like everyone else. Therefore, they ultimately define themselves by the gulf between themselves and their students. As a consequence, there is no incentive for the guru to teach his/

her students to trust their own innate wisdom. Not to mention there is a financial incentive in keeping students coming back for yet more levels of widom and esoteric techniques meant to take them yet higher and higher on a ladder that is supposed to lead to enlightenment. What results from this relationship is a lifetime of students doing nothing more than grasping for something beyond themselves.

Today's yoga must wean itself off its addiction to the guru/student dynamic. It is critical in the practice of CHY that facilitators allow participants to arrive at their own truths through energetic practice. CHY facilitators should have *Equality of Presence*, meaning that they should try to be as much a part of the practice as everyone else. It also means that one of the goals of facilitators should be to help calibrate the participant's own energetic barometer for personal truth. As a consequence, no one's truth has precedent over any one else's regardless of their title, notoriety, or years of practice.

Group configurations

Recognition of resonance happens initially with the pairing of participants back-to-back, and will prove further enhanced whenever you can position participants male-to-female, to balance Shiva and Shakti energies.

First, duos perform the Cobras, individually raising or lowering their pitch until they achieve mutual resonance. After the pairing, the same sequence is repeat with trios. There should be at least one member of the opposite sex represented in each group of three. Each triad is seated with their backs arranged in a triangular fashion as shown in this top view in figure 9-10 (next page):

When the trio achieves resonance they are ready

Collective Heart Yoga

to be positioned in the same balanced pattern with all the trios arranged in a sacred geometry. The figure 9-11 on the following page shows the largest single configuration for (18) participants. The six-pointed star is the traditional symbol for the heart. The downward-pointed triangle represents Shiva's masculine energy. The upward-pointed triangle represents Shakti's female energy.

Figure 9-16 The cobra breathing triad configuration

If there are more there are more or less than the optimum 18 participants, there are a myriad of star patterns and other positions to maximize the group energy flow, as fully illustrated in Appendix A.

The Science and Practice of Manifesting Unity Consciousness

Figure 9-17 Configuration of 18 participants employing sacred geometry

Please note that certain numbers of participants do not lend themselves mathematically to sacred geometries that integrate solely as triads. Be assured, a few well-positioned pairs will not take away from the effectiveness of the session. Six is one perfect number for pairs and trios. However, as few as two solo practitioners can come together back-to-back and will certainly manifest far more collective energy than either could accomplish alone.

In an earlier definition of resonance, the example was confined to only the sound produced by the group mantras during the last phase of the practice. The resonant harmonies of the collective mantras will probably not go beyond the practice room.

Yet a deeper meaning of resonance reveals that, in a coherent system, one object may set any other object into vibration providing it shares a resonant frequency. The most accessible example is what happens when you strike a tuning fork of a certain frequency and bring it in the field of another tuned to a sympathetic frequency. The other tuning fork will also begin to vibrate even though it has not been struck.

The resonance achieved in the room during the Yoga of Collective Manifestation is only an initiatory vibration intended to evoke another sympathetic frequency far beyond our normal senses' capacity to measure. This type of resonance occurs in the frequency of thought and intention, a range higher than light which extends far beyond the practice room.

Through the practice of Collective Heart Yoga the collective resonant frequencies are amplified and focused in a room filled with individual hearts joined together with one coherent intention for the healing of Mother Earth. As instructed earlier, participants agree to set aside special interests and personal issues to manifest pure, child-like, unconditional healing heart energy, which will then be projected to resonate with identical frequencies within the collective unconscious, thereby affecting us each and all, touching everyone everywhere at once.

Healing with the power of our Collective Heart.

Namaste,
Jude R. Johnson
Asheville, NC

References

1. Sunyata, S. *Notes on Karana Kriyas*.
2. Harish J. (1988) *Tools for Tantra.* Rochester, Vt. Destiny Books
3. Melchizedek, D. (2003) Living in the Heart. Flagstaff, AZ. Light Technology Publishing.
4. Ipsalu Tantra workshop handout
5. Saraswati, S. *Wand of Perpetual Youth: T'ai Chi Ruler.* workshop handout.
6. Adapted from Lisa Renee: http://www.energeticsynthesis.com/index.php?option=com_content&view=article&id=50&Itemid=85

Appendix
Alternate Group Configurations for Cobra Breathing

9 Participants

8 Participants

7 Participants

6 Participants

Collective Heart Yoga

5 Participants

4 Partipants

3 Participants

2 Participants

About the Author

I have been both a student and teacher for as long as I remember. My last teaching assignment was as an Associate Professor. Yet despite over a decade of successful university teaching and the "security" of tenure, I chose to resign, blaming the beginning of the end on a Kundalini awakening I experienced in my late 30's. There was no place in the curriculum to integrate the spiritual wisdom I had attained from years of worldly travel and the extensive study of many forms of yoga with a particular emphasis on kriya yoga as taught by Sunyata Saraswati and Bodhi Avinasha to name a few.

Strangely enough, the day after I actually submitted my letter of resignation to Mercer, I started receiving what could

The Science and Practice of Manifesting Unity Consciousness

only be described as downloads during my cobra breath meditations. The downloads made little sense at first until I realized that it all had to do with manifestation on a collective level. The basic outline of the practice was made apparent. I filled in the gaps with appropriate practices from my years of training as well as new practices that were delivered during meditation.

After over a year of deep meditation, research, and writing, Collective Heart Yoga (CHY) became a reality. The only guidelines I received concerning the dissemination of the practice was that it be shared completely, openly, and affordably

When not working on CHY, I nurtured another spiritual love child called EnlightenmentNetwork.com (EN), an extensive collection of profoundly entertaining videos including original video productions such as the talk shows, Quantum Encounters, and Health in the Spiritual Body. In the six years of EN, we have created over 20 original productions that include everything from instructional DVDs to interviews with cutting-edge authors and spiritual practitioners. We continue to help authentic spiritual teachers get their message to a larger number of hearts via video and the internet.

I currently call the magical city of Asheville, NC my beloved base camp. I travel extensively, lecturing and facilitating open workshops for Collective Heart Yoga. For more information on upcoming speaking engagements or workshops please check out www.CollectiveHeartYoga.org.

The Science and Practice of Manifesting Unity Consciousness

Index

Symbols

9/11 attacks 103
26 thousand year cycle 23, 93

A

Abundance 53
acoustic archetypes 10, 126
Anahata 43, 44, 99, 108, 148, 150
Angel Oracle Cards 114
angels 109, 114
apocalypse 130
Archangels 114, 115
archetypes 50, 100, 153
Armour 38, 39
Marc Arno 20
avatars 109, 161, 163
Bodhi Avinasha 180

B

Babaji 110
Andrew Beers 7, 21
Bhramari Pranayama 12, 148
Big Bang 29, 46, 117
Biophotonic coherence 9, 62
Neils Bohr 58
Lawrence Buchine 151

C

Carl Calleman 29, 117
Catholic church 56
Edgar Cayce 9, 105
Chakra Chromatics 151
chakras 11, 25, 26, 70, 76, 79, 80, 95, 99
Teilhard de Chardin 117
chladni disk 95
Deepak Chopra 74
Christ Consciousness Grid 10, 11, 117, 128, 129

Cobra Breath
 Cosmic Cobra Breath 21
 Emanating Heart Cobra 26, 159, 161
 Manifestation Cobra 26, 158, 159, 163
 Tantric Cobra Breath 21
collective unconscious. 99, 100, 117, 165
Conception Vessel 143
Copernicus 56
Cortisol 42
Cosmic Child 50, 153, 165
Cosmic Convergence 15, 130
Cosmic Father 50, 153
Course in Miracles 81

D

Annette Deyhle 20, 107
DHEA 42
divine emissary 9, 109, 111, 112
DNA 11, 38, 46, 57, 64, 65, 66, 67, 69
dodecahedron grid 127, 128

E

ego 100
Albert Einstein 57, 58
entrainment 94
eye gazing 12, 157, 158

F

facilitator 161, 163
Fa-tsang 85
forgiveness 28, 70, 71, 75, 77, 78, 81, 113
Buckminster Fuller 11, 126

G

Global Coherence Initiative 9, 20, 28, 39, 102, 107
Gnostic Gospels 70
Daniel Goleman 72
Governer's Channel 143
gratitude 8, 21, 42, 43
Gregg Braden 20, 67

Group Unity Decree 133

H

Harmonic Convergence 130
David Hawkins 9, 91, 92
Health in the Spiritual Body 180
Higher Self 112
Hong Saw Breath 79, 89
Chen Hsi-I 143
Humming Bee Breath. *See* Bhramari Pranayama

I

Immortals Wand. *See* T'ai Chí Ruler
inner smile 133
inner-smile meditation 133
Ipsalu Tantra 18, 171

J

Jesus 75, 77, 110, 111, 113, 161, 163
Connie Johnson 19, 111
Carl Jung 28, 100

K

Kabbalah 31
  Tree of Life 151
kalchakra 86
Kalipatra 48
Karana Kriyas 136, 137
Karma 76
Kechari Mudra 143
Ko Hum meditation 106
Krishna 113
Kuan Yin 113
Kundalini 13, 20

L

Long Count Calendar 10, 29, 117, 120, 123, 130
Ian Lungold 117

M

Earth's magnetic field 40, 103, 104
Matthew Manning 65
mantra 96
  bija 96, 99
  tibetan seed 96, 99
Mayan Calendar 10, 117, 122, 131
Mayan Long Count Calendar 10, 29, 117, 120, 123, 130
Rollin Mcraty 20, 65, 69, 107
Lynne McTaggart 20
medulla 134
Mother Earth 21, 30, 33, 46, 49, 50, 54, 100, 116, 132, 153, 154, 160, 162, 170
mouth of God 134

N

nadis 12, 153
Nadi Shadhona 106, 152
Roger Nelson 103
New Age 33
Issaac, Newton 57, 58
Nonlocality 9, 58

O

Barack Obama 104
Open Source 26

P

Phi ratio 11, 66
Platonic Solids 11, 127
pranayam 25
Ptolemy 56

Q

quantum 26, 47, 57, 58, 59, 68, 69, 72, 73, 74, 88, 118
Quantum Encounters 180
quantum entanglement 59

R

Glen Rein 64
resonance 14, 95, 96, 97, 98, 165, 166, 167, 169, 170
Roving Heart Beat 148, 149

S

sacred geometry 3, 11, 12, 17, 28, 98, 168, 169
Sacred Space Meditation 50, 153
Valerie Sadyrin 65
saints 109
Sunyata Saraswati 21, 45
Helmut Schmidt 85
The Secret 33
Service 8, 23, 29, 30, 33
Shakti 96, 97, 100, 108, 143, 153, 167, 168
Shiva 96, 97, 100, 108, 143, 153, 167, 168
solar cycle 105
Henry Stapp 85
Star of David 3, 17
sunspots 105

T

T'ai Chí Ruler 136, 143, 171
tantra 161, 163
tetrahedron 17
The Secret 8, 33
Toroidal Antenna Model 67
Toroidal Field 11, 52

U

unconscious 100
Unity Breath 50, 153

V

Vladimir Vernadsky 117
vibration 10, 25, 26, 30, 45, 52, 53, 94, 96, 127, 148, 149, 156, 157, 170
Dirk Vorenkamp 85

W

Witness consciousness 8, 44

Y

Yantra 25
Young's slit experiment 59

Z

Zen Buddhism 82
Zohar 31

The Science and Practice of Manifesting Unity Consciousness

www.ingramcontent.com/pod-product-compliance
Lightning Source LLC
Chambersburg PA
CBHW062217080426
42734CB00010B/1929